THE ISLE OF MAN
COASTAL PATH

ABOUT THE AUTHOR

Aileen Evans, now retired after a career in teaching and book production, has enjoyed a lifelong love of the outdoors. She has climbed, walked, skied and camped in many parts of Europe and North America and considers the Isle of Man a favourite which continually draws her to return.

She prefers to linger on a walk, allowing time to appreciate views, to enjoy flowers and wildlife, and delve into things of historical interest.

Aileen has always enjoyed adventure sports and sampled most, including pot-holing, wild-water canoeing and alpine mountaineering. She still particularly enjoys rock climbing and exploring little-known places away from mainstream tourist areas. Recently, with encouragement from her grandson, she has taken up mountain biking.

Some of Aileen's more memorable tours include cross- country ski-backpacking in France, walking across the remote interior of Iceland and a trek to Iceland's North Cape, and completing the Tour of Mont Blanc and the Alpine Pass Route.

At home in Lancashire, with her husband, Brian, and collie, Meg, she enjoys her garden, particularly the visiting birds.

THE ISLE OF MAN COASTAL PATH

RAAD NY FOILLAN – THE WAY OF THE GULL

Includes also
the Millennium Way and
the Bayr ny Skeddan – The Herring Way

Aileen Evans

2 POLICE SQUARE, MILNTHORPE, CUMBRIA LA7 7PY
www.cicerone.co.uk

© Aileen Evans 1988, 1998, 2004

Third edition 2004 (reprinted 2007 and 2009 (with updates))
ISBN-10: 1 85284 400 0
ISBN-13: 978 1 85284 400 4
Second edition 1998
ISBN: 1 85284 277 6
First edition 1988

A catalogue record for this book is available from the British Library.

Printed by KHL Printing, Singapore

Acknowledgements

I would like to thank the many kind people of the island who have helped me along the way and with the writing of this guide. Thanks also to Anna Hemy, Maxwell Collister, Wendy Taylor of the Department of Tourism and John Callister, Countryside Warden, Manx National Heritage.

For photographs, the maps and drawings I must thank my husband, Brian, who patiently packed up at a moment's notice to follow me round the island.

Front cover: Port Erin Bay and Bradda Head

CONTENTS

Coming over the moor above Black Head, with Bay Stacka below

PREFACE

The Raad ny Foillan (The Way of the Gull) is a 98 mile footpath around the coastline of the Isle of Man. This long-distance footpath was set up in 1986 to mark the island's Heritage Year. In its journey round the Isle of Man the Raad ny Foillan offers a variety of scenery, from the rugged cliffs and mountain moorland in the south, to the glens, beaches and dunes of the north. It wends its way through several nature reserves and along a disused railway. It passes scenes of historical interest, colourful fishing villages and peaceful havens. It takes to the road in several places, yet these country lanes have their own charm and little traffic. The single stretch of main road is of short duration. The footpath is never far from the sea or the cry of the gull. It is suitable for the gentle walker to do in short day-walk sections, for the dedicated backpacker, and for the fit fell-runner to set up his own personal record for the delightful circuit of this beautiful island.

The idea of a coastal footpath was first promoted by a former Governor of the Island, Sir Ambrose Flux Dunas, himself a keen rambler. There was no legislation similar to the Parks and Countryside Act in the UK, but he paved the way for the 1961 Rights of Way Act. By 1973 maps were prepared and the task of waymarking and improving sections of the coastal path began. Dave Woods, the Rights of Way Officer, took on the task and in the Heritage Year, 1986, the Raad ny Foillan was opened.

In this guide I have tried to introduce you to the Isle of Man as I have found it. As a child I visited Douglas, and returned with memories of seaside bustle, horse-drawn trams and a lurching ship. My next visit was as a rock climber, which fixed memories of a rugged coastline with crags and secret coves. A third visit was as a backpacker to walk the coastal path. It far exceeded my expectations. After the first day, gone were all my preconceived ideas of roaring motorbikes sporting dayglow stickers. I came away with pictures of primroses in Glen Maye, the sunset turning the surf to gold and the wet noses of the seals as they questioned my presence so close to their domain. I hope that as you follow the Manx footpaths you will collect as many happy memories as I did.

The Introduction to the guide covers the practicalities necessary to organise your 'expedition', as well as interesting things to be seen on the way and their background.

The description of the Raad ny Foillan sets out the circuit in stages, the longest being 15½ miles, the shortest 7 miles. The fast walker may wish to complete two stages per day, while those progressing at a more leisurely pace may decide to amble along and take in the diverting attractions along the way. I chose to begin at Douglas simply because I arrived by boat and was keen to literally step from the quay onto the footpath. As the way borders Ronaldsway Airport the starting point is a matter of choice and presents no problem.

The footpath is waymarked and so, together with the information given in this guide, should enable the walker to progress easily and, if adverse conditions arise, safely.

The guide also covers the island's first long-distance footpath, the Millennium Way (see page 127), which was opened in 1979 to celebrate the millennium year of Tynwald. This follows an ancient route from Ramsey to Castletown. The Bayr ny Skeddan (the Herring Way, see page 139), established in 1986, is an old trade route from Peel to Castletown.

Although the Isle of Man sits snuggly in the Irish Sea surrounded by the British Isles, it is different from the rest of the United Kingdom. UK money is accepted, but your change may become mixed with the Manx currency, which is legal tender only on the island. The island government also issue their own stamps. If you post anything on the island, it must have a Manx stamp. The Isle of Man is part of the mainland telephone network and has good cellphone coverage.

The pace of life is easy; people seem to have time to talk. I obtained some helpful advice from a gang of commissioners (council workers) who were laying a hedge. A fisherman mending his nets was only too pleased to inform me of the state of the Irish Sea and its fish over the last ten years. (Things are vastly improved, by the way.)

Although the early Manxmen were of Celtic origin, Man was part of the Norwegian Kingdom of the Hebrides until 1266. It is now a self-governing Crown Dependency, the Lieutenant-Governor being the Queen's representative on the island.

The legislature, The Tynwald, has two branches. The first is the Legislative Council that comprises the Bishop, the Attorney and eight members. The other branch is the House of Keys, which has twenty-four elected members. The Isle of Man has a special relationship with the European Community but does not contribute to, nor receive, funds from the EEC budget.

Douglas is the capital of the island, a position held by Castletown until 1869. It is the home of Manx Radio, which was the first commercial radio station in the British Isles.

An important difference which affects the Raad ny Foillan is that campervans, but not caravans, are allowed on the island, thus it remains free from the coastal developments which have so despoiled much of Britain's coastline. The Manx treat their coastline as a prized asset and are making every effort to maintain its present beauty. Long-distance walkers will inevitably compare the Raad ny Foillan favourably with the South West Peninsula Path of Devon and Cornwall, where huge static caravan sites often dominate the scenery.

Important to the walker is that inns and hotels are open all day Monday to Saturday. Most serve food and you can sample the real Manx ale. An ancient law prohibits the use of any substitutes for malt, sugar or hops, so you do get the real local brew. The Manx ice-cream is the genuine article too and has received the accolade of the highest award in Britain. I cannot vouch for the ale, but I can definitely give the thumbs up to the ice-cream.

Aileen Evans
Preston 1987

Updates to the Second Edition
Little has changed to the footpath itself except a short, though significant, re-routing of the path to include an impressive stretch of coastline to Niarbyl.

Aileen Evans
Preston 1998

Updates to the Third Edition
The travel information, accommodation, campsite list and service details have been brought up to date. Any additions to the route are included.

Aileen Evans
Preston 2004

Map Key

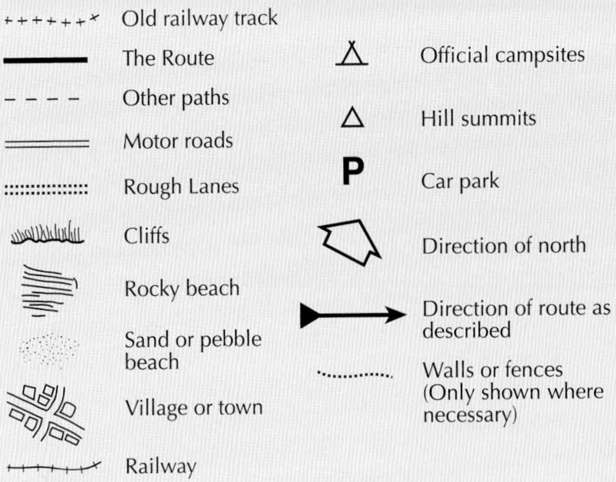

+++++××	Old railway track		
▬▬▬	The Route	Λ	Official campsites
- - - -	Other paths	△	Hill summits
═══	Motor roads	**P**	Car park
:::::::::::	Rough Lanes		
(cliffs)	Cliffs	⬠	Direction of north
(rocky)	Rocky beach	➤	Direction of route as described
(sand)	Sand or pebble beach	....	Walls or fences (Only shown where necessary)
(village)	Village or town		
++++××	Railway		

Note: (w/m) used throughout the text denotes a waymark

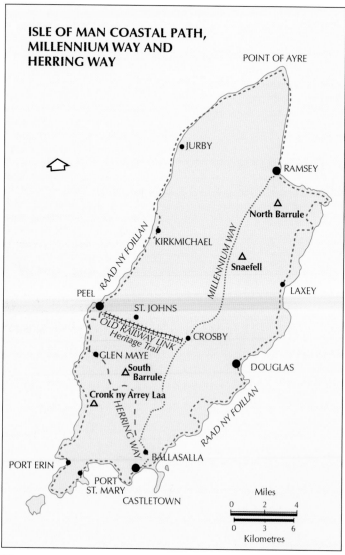

ISLE OF MAN COASTAL PATH,
MILLENNIUM WAY AND
HERRING WAY

POINT OF AYRE

• JURBY

• RAMSEY

△ North Barrule

RAAD NY FOILLAN

• KIRKMICHAEL

MILLENNIUM WAY

△ Snaefell

PEEL • • LAXEY

ST. JOHNS •

OLD RAILWAY LINK
Heritage Trail

• CROSBY

• GLEN MAYE

△ South Barrule

Cronk ny Arrey Laa
△

• DOUGLAS

HERRING WAY

RAAD NY FOILLAN

PORT ERIN •

• BALLASALLA

PORT
ST. MARY

CASTLETOWN

Miles
0   2   4

0   3   6
Kilometres

INTRODUCTION

HOW TO GET THERE

The Isle of Man Steam Packet Company has regular sailings from Heysham and Liverpool to Douglas, and from Belfast and Dublin to Douglas (summer service only). Car parking is available at the dock.

For details of timetables and fares consult the Isle of Man Steam Packet Company (tel: 08705 523 523; online: www.steam-packet.com).

- All boats are drive on/off car ferries.
- Bicycles are transported free.
- Dogs are allowed, and a dedicated area of the lounge is set aside.
- Trailer caravans are not permitted on the island without a permit. Self-propelled motor caravans are welcome, as are tenting campers.

By air there is a daily service to Ronaldsway from the following airports: Belfast City, Birmingham, Blackpool, Bristol, Brussels, Dublin, East Midlands, Edinburgh, Glasgow, Guernsey, Jersey, Leeds/Bradford, Liverpool, London City, London Gatwick, London Luton, London Stansted, Manchester and Newcastle. Note: there is no service into London Heathrow.

The coastal footpath is within a mile of the island's airport (tel: 01624 821600; www.iomguide.com).

The Sea Cat arrives at Douglas harbour

THE BEST TIME TO WALK

Everyone hopes for good weather, and you can increase your chances to some extent by looking at the past meteorological reports (see also 'Climate', below). May and June stand out as the months with a good sunshine average and little rainfall. The holiday season begins in June and is virtually over by mid-September, yet in the middle of the season I met very few people on the footpath, except around the Sound Cafe where tourists were taking the air within sight of the car park. Most walkers that I met were Manx and were pleased to see a 'foreigner' enjoying their coastline. Spring brings flowers to the glens and migrant birds to the beaches. Late summer glows with the dwarf gorse in flower, heather in bloom and sunsets on the west coast that make an extra amble around in the twilight worthwhile.

If there is a time of year to avoid it is late May, early June and early September: the weeks of the motorcycle and car rallies. At these times the ferries, accommodation and campsites are fully booked. The closure of roads for these and other events does not inconvenience the Raad ny Foillan walker, but the Millennium Way and the Herring Way will be affected.

Having said all this, I walked the Millennium Way in the first weekend of the TT practices. I met one other walker, a small group of scouts cooking bacon and beans, and a horse rider. I camped in delectable surroundings and the weather was superb.

A provisional list of events for the year is published by the Isle of Man Department of Tourism and Leisure (tel: 01624 686766; website: www.gov.im/tourism; e-mail: tourism@gov.im; Weather Check: 01696 888300).

ACCOMMODATION

Current lists of hotels, bed and breakfast, hostel accommodation and campsites are available from the Department of Tourism and Leisure. They have prepared a list of accommodation near the Raad ny Foillan specially for the walker (see Appendix 4: IOM Coastal Footpath accommodation list).

PUBLIC TRANSPORT

Tel: 01624 662525; Website: www.isleofman.com/gettingaround/msr2003.htm

The Isle of Man is well served with public transport. Bus routes, an electric railway and a steam railway cover the island.

The Isle of Man Passenger Transport publishes a booklet of official timetables that is available from the Information Bureau at the Douglas Sea Terminal, at any bus terminal, and at local Tourist or Commissioners' Information Offices. It is useful to obtain this timetable before planning your trip as, for example, the circular routes from Ramsey via Jurby, Bride,

The Manx Electric Railway is a familiar sight

Smeale, Andreas and Jurby may influence your choice of accommodation.

Tickets described as 'inter-available' can be purchased for bus, train and tram travel. These can be bought from retail transport shops in Douglas, Peel, Port Erin and Ramsey, or you can pay on the bus in the usual manner. Explorer tickets may be purchased on the island or in advance for unlimited travel by bus or train for one, three, five or seven consecutive days.

The steam train runs from Douglas (Bank Hill Station is at the southern end of the harbour) to Port Erin. The whole line is within easy reach of the Raad ny Foillan. Stations along the line are: Port Soderick, Santon (by request), Ballasalla, Ronaldsway (by request), Castletown, Port St Mary, Port Erin. Trains run Easter and May–September.

The electric railway runs from Douglas (Derby Castle Terminus is at the northern end of the promenade) to Ramsey. There are numerous request halts along the way, the main ones being Groudle, Baldrine, South Cape, Laxey, Dhoon, Ballaglass, Ballajora and Ramsey. The electric railway runs from 7th April to 26th October.

From Laxey Station the Snaefell Mountain Railway makes the journey to the summit.

Bus services are more frequent in summer, May–September, when 30 routes criss-cross the island. All the towns and large villages are on a bus route, and special services run in the summer to Cregneish and The Sound from Port Erin.

There is another form of public transport which you may find irresistible if you have blisters on the

13

Horse-drawn tram on Douglas promenade

last lap – the horse-drawn trams clip-clopping their way along Douglas promenade!

CLIMATE

The climate of the Isle of Man can be summed up as being milder than that of its UK neighbours. The influence of the surrounding relatively warm sea is the major factor. In winter the temperatures seldom fall below freezing. The 42 degrees isotherm, after passing through the Isle of Wight, swings northward to capture the Isle of Man. In summer the sea exerts a cooling influence and the island enjoys the pleasant gap between the 58 degrees and 60 degrees isotherms. The annual amount of rainfall on the coastline is 30–40ins. per year, most of this falling in the winter

months. As can be expected, it is heavier on the mountains. The wind often lifts the clouds over the coastline, leaving it dry, whilst inland the hills are swathed in cloud. The prevailing wind is south-west. This is a consideration in planning your route. If you tackle the walk clockwise the length of the west coast will put any breeze at your back, then as you turn the Point of Ayre to come south the cliffs and mountains will provide shelter.

Another facet of the weather is the sea mist. The air over the sea can be saturated with water vapour. A drop of only one degree in temperature can result in the condensation of suspended vapour causing mist in the surrounding air. Thus mist can roll in from the sea with little warning. Douglas can be covered in mist while the rest of the island is bathed in sunshine.

The Isle of Man has an excellent bonus to offer. The clean air of the island supports 500 varieties of lichens to testify to its purity.

TIDES AND TIMES

[Isle of Man Coastguard, tel: 01624 661664]

The sea makes such a major contribution to the Raad ny Foillan that it is to your advantage to learn a little about its ways. Things that seem obvious and familiar to those fortunate enough to live near the sea may be amusing, but could soon become alarming, to those who make the odd visit to the sea and are not familiar with its various moods.

The tide flows up the Irish Sea in a northerly direction, bending round the Point of Ayre to take an easterly direction along the Galloway coast. The ebb flows at 2½ knots from Galloway south back down the Irish Sea.

The tidal flow reaches Liverpool at roughly the same time as the Isle of Man, the tidal differences in time and height on Liverpool being shown in the table on the following page.

The times and heights of the tides for Standard Port – Liverpool can be found easily in the national daily newspapers or by studying one of the nautical almanacs.

The tidal stream changes direction every 6 hours. The ebb usually

Ballaugh Beach and Jurby Head

At Point of Ayre: beyond the foghorn the tide race is in full ebb

runs longer than 6 hours, whilst the flood runs slightly less than six hours, low tide being 6hrs 10mins after high tide. This results in advancing the time of high water and low water by ³/₄hr every 24 hours.

The strength of the tidal stream varies daily because of the position of the moon. The tide height and range is greatest at spring tides. Spring tides occur two days after new and full moons; neap tides fortnightly halfway between spring tides, two days after the first and last quarters of the moon. Spring tide height at Liverpool (MHWS

9.3m) is considered high at 9 metres but twice a year makes 10 metres. This is a result of the influence of the sun and the moon, and occurs at the vernal equinox (21st March) and the autumnal equinox (21st September). The tide races at The Sound and Point of Ayre run at 3–3.5 knots.

Another feature of interest to walkers on the Raad ny Foillan is the influence the wind has on the height of the waves. I had heard of freak waves arriving from nowhere, but had never fully appreciated the extra wave height generated even by a modest breeze.

TIDAL DIFFERENCES FOR ISLE OF MAN COMPARED TO LIVERPOOL				
	Mean High Water		Mean Low Water	
	Time Diff. H. Min	Ht. Diff. m.MHWS	Time Diff. H. Min	Ht. Diff. m.MLWS
Ramsey	+0.05	-1.9	-0.05	-0.6
Laxey	0.10	-2.0	-0.20	-0.3
Peel	-0.05	-4.1	-0.25	-0.9

(from Macmillan Reeds Nautical Almanac 2003)

BEAUFORT WIND SCALE

Scale	mph		Ht of waves (metres)	Appearance
0	less than 1	calm	–	mirror
1	1–3	light air	0.0	ripples
2	4–6	light breeze	0.1	small wavelets
3	7–10	gentle breeze	0.4	large wavelets
4	11–16	mod. breeze	1.0	small waves
5	17–21	fresh breeze	2.0	mod. waves, horses
6	22–27	strong breeze	3.0	large waves many horses, spray
7	28–33	near gale	4.0	sea heaps
8	34–40	gale	5.5	mod. high waves
9	41–47	severe gale	7.0	high waves
10	48–55	storm	9.0	
11	56–63	violentstorm	11.0	
12	64+	hurricane	14.0	

The following chart will help you gauge the height of the waves on the sea and the extra amount of water they may throw at you above the normal high tide. I cannot resist the fascination of waves dashing over the rocks and exploding against the cliffs, a real bonus to be enjoyed in bad weather – from a safe distance of course.

MAPS AND COMPASSES

The maps in this guide are sufficient to enable you to walk the Raad ny Foillan, but you will need to step off the route from time to time. A map of the island will help you to obtain the maximum enjoyment, replenish your supplies and be sure of your nearest point of help in the case of an emergency. Along with the map you may need to take a compass (and know how to use it).

The Official Tourist Map of the island contains town plans at a scale of 1:60,000.

The Isle of Man Public Rights of Way and Outdoor Leisure Maps North and South marks the Raad ny Foillan and the shorter footpaths, the Millennium Way, the Bayr ny Skeddan, and the the Heritage Trail (10½ miles from Douglas to Peel along the route of the old railway), at a scale of 1:25,000. It is a wonderful map for detail that you can enjoy in your armchair afterwards. Almost every cove and headland is named, every field drawn and places of historical interest identified. The contour lines, imaginary lines passing through all places of equal height, are at 100ft intervals.

By roughly orientating the map you will be able to identify the mountains and surrounding countryside. The top of the map is north. Place your compass on one of the vertical grid lines on your map and rotate the map until the grid line is parallel with the compass needle.

This method is approximate and is not good enough if you are enveloped suddenly by a thick mist. In this case:

- Place your compass on the map with the rotating capsule turned so that the north arrow on the dial is in its correct position at 0 (or 360 degrees), with the whole compass pointing north to the top of the map. The grid lines will help you to do this.

- Slowly rotate the map keeping the compass firmly in place, still pointing to the top of the map (north), until the compass needle swings and points to the magnetic north which is 3 deg. 10 mins. west of true north (2003). Your map is now set and you should be able to follow the desired direction.

The Ordnance Survey map of the Isle of Man – Landranger 1:50,000 sheet No.95 – is a revised issue 1987, but the marking of the three long-distance footpaths lacks detail.

GEOLOGY

If you have no interest in geology when you begin the Raad ny Foillan you are sure to have your interest

The miners' packhorse bridge over the infant Sulby river

Contorted strata in an isolated bay below the Marine Drive at The Whing

aroused in the first few miles. If you have a general basic knowledge, you will become excited at the strata on view. If you are a geologist you will be continually left behind and will have to restrain yourself from loading yourself and your companions with samples! As you progress from Douglas clockwise round the island you will be introduced to rocks from the very oldest to the most recent at the Point of Ayre, then as you move down the east coast you will be able to recognise them again as old friends.

The Isle of Man has few crags inland, but the stone used in the old local walls and buildings, and the vegetation cover, will give you clues to the nature of the underlying rocks. At the coast, however, the rock strata is exposed, washed and ready for inspection.

The Isle of Man is part of the Irish Sea horst. In layman's terms a horst is a ridge pushed up between two great faults (cracks in the earth). In Cambro-Ordovician times, layers of muds and silts known as the Manx or Barrule slates were deposited. Movements in the earth's crust caused subsidence, which was followed by marine deposition, when the carboniferous limestones were deposited. Next was a period of uplift and folding. The movement produced the Irish Sea horst, the plateau-like area. This horst extends from Ireland to the English Lake District, the Isle of Man being the central part protruding above the waters of the Irish Sea. The folded Barrule slates can be seen from the Marine Drive, where they give rise to magnificent coastal scenery. In the Tertiary period dykes (vertical cracks filled from below with molten

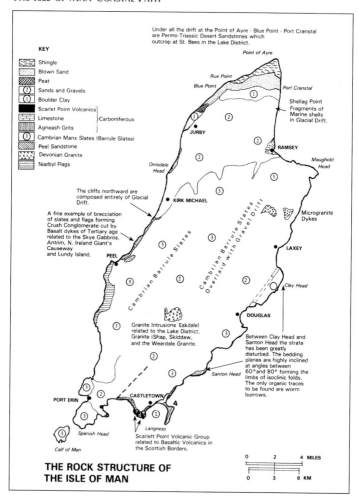

KEY

▨	Shingle
▨	Blown Sand
▨	Peat
②	Sands and Gravels
①	Boulder Clay
▪	Scarlet Point Volcanics
▨	Limestone } Carboniferous
▨	Agneash Grits
①	Cambrian Manx Slates (Barrule Slates)
▨	Peel Sandstone
▨	Devonian Granite
▨	Niarbyl Flags

Under all the drift at the Point of Ayre - Blue Point - Port Cranstal are Permo-Triassic Desert Sandstones which outcrop at St. Bees in the Lake District.

Point of Ayre

Rue Point

Blue Point

Port Cranstal

Shellag Point
Fragments of Marine shells in Glacial Drift.

JURBY

RAMSEY

Orrisdale Head

Maughold Head

The cliffs northward are composed entirely of Glacial Drift.

KIRK MICHAEL

Microgranite Dykes

A fine example of brecciation of slates and flags forming Crush Conglomerate cut by Basalt dykes of Tertiary age related to the Skye Gabbros, Antrim, N. Ireland Giant's Causeway and Lundy Island.

PEEL

Cambrian Barrule Slates

Cambrian Barrule Slates Overlaid with Gravel Drift

LAXEY

Clay Head

DOUGLAS

Granite Intrusions Eskdale) related to the Lake District. Granite (Shap, Skiddaw, and the Weardale Granite.

Between Clay Head and Santon Head the strata has been greatly disturbed. The bedding planes are highly inclined at angles between 60° and 80° forming the limbs of isoclinic folds. The only organic traces to be found are worm burrows.

Santon Head

PORT ERIN

CASTLETOWN

Langness

Spanish Head

Scarlett Point Volcanic Group related to Basaltic Volcanics in the Scottish Borders.

Calf of Man

THE ROCK STRUCTURE OF THE ISLE OF MAN

0	2	4 MILES
0	3	6 KM

basalt) occurred in profusion, cutting through the strata and resulting in sudden changes of colour and texture.

During the Ice Ages glaciers covered the island. As they moved south they carried with them large boulders from Scotland, which were

Fine examples of slates, flags and dykes are found on the coast north of Peel

subsequently deposited as erratics. Many of these have been used in buildings. As the glaciers crossed the sea they scooped up and carried marine deposits from the sea bed. As the ice melted, sands, gravels and boulder clays were abandoned. During its passage the ice planed away some areas of the Manx slates to expose the underlying granite.

In recent geological times raised beaches were formed in the north of the island. Accumulations of peat and blown sand are still in the process of settling, completing the geological picture of the island for

LOCATIONS OF VISIBLE GEOLOGICAL STRATA		
Recent	Blown sand	The Ayres, Jurby, Andreas, Poyllvaaish, Langness
	Peat	In beds; on the hills and mountains
	Alluvium and river drift	Southern plain
	Marine raised beach	Derby Haven, Cass-ny-Hawin
Glacial	Sand and gravels	The Bride hills and scattered mounds
	Boulder clay and rubble drift	Blue Point, south of Port Cranstal
Carboniferous	Limestone series	Castletown, Scarlett
	Basement sandstone	Peel
	Basement conglomerate	Langness, Ballasalla, Peel
Upper Cambrian	Manx slates Barrule slates, Agneash grits, Crush Conglomerates, Lonan and Niarbyl flags	South of a line Ramsey to Kirk Michael
Igneous Rocks	Granite	Santon, Foxdale, Dhoon
	See map on page 20 for locations.	

you to examine at close quarters from the footpath.

The visible geological strata in evidence are shown on the table on the table below.

NATURE ALONG THE FOOTPATHS

One of the delights of the Raad ny Foillan is the contrast of the vast expanse of sea and sky with the intimate environment of the plants at your feet and birds skimming over your head.

The mild, damp climate is without extremes of temperature, but the continually changing base rocks and the soil they support must be the main factor contributing to the variety of plant and animal life you are likely to see on the way.

Plants

The book *The Flowering Plants of the Isle of Man* counts 38 varieties of fern and fern allies, 853 flowering plants and 9 types of conifer to be found on the island. Some are very rare and best left to prosper in their secret havens. Others show off their flowers, generously lining the footpath, and a limited description of what to expect, and where, is given below.

The mountains and headlands are mainly of Barrule slate. The highest mountain is Snaefell (2036ft) and is rather low for mountain species, although a few can be seen. The peaty soil supports a mixture of gorse and heather. The common gorse was introduced for fodder, fuel and reinforcing the banked hedgerows. The dwarf gorse, which flowers in the late summer, is native to the island. Bracken

Heather and dwarf gorse adorn the moors

and cotton grass take no finding, but the tiny asphodel, white and yellow bedstraw, sundew, and the violet and vetches that seem to grow everywhere need a little more careful attention if you are to enjoy them.

The glens, sheltered from the winds, are veritable greenhouses, and the common trees and plants which grow there appear more vibrant. The stems are taller, the colours brighter, scents unrecognised hang in the air, ferns and mosses take on an artistic grace previously unnoticed. Palm trees and fuchsia grow with the abandoned air of a native plant, and it is often difficult to know where cultivation ends and nature takes over. The lanes encountered are often between high stone and sod walls. Overgrown, the stones are

Orchid on Spanish Head

often hidden by a cascade of flowers best seen in the spring – bluebells, celandine, primroses, yellow poppies and violets intermingled with buds of ramsons, red campion, and greater stitchwort, with the wild rose and sweet briar patiently waiting for the summer. Where the stone is on view, ground ivy, stonecrop and pennywort do their best to clothe it, with the rue-leaved saxifrage and herb Robert adding their own distinctive colours.

The limestone of Scarlett Point has its own nature trail and Visitor Centre, where a small yet comprehensive booklet is available. Flowers of the limestone and those loving the proximity of the sea abound. Sea thrift, white sea campion, buttercup and bird's-foot trefoil cannot be missed, but just beyond the coastguard station, the minute mauve and white flowers of the sand spurrey and the purple thyme can be easily overlooked. The spring squill abounds amongst the short turf, and on the basalt dykes lichens can be examined. The lichen is a dual plant – a fungus, determining the shape, living with an alga, its chlorophyll making the food. The two varieties on the basalt are as different as chalk and cheese. *Romalina Siliquosa is* the tall grey spiky one; *Lecanora Atra* is the flat, frill-like orange one. These are only two of the many varieties on the island.

The sand and gravels of the north are still mobile and settling according to the whim of the weather. This is an area of unique scientific interest, and

Sea holly at Rue Point

as you would expect its welfare is guarded by the Ayres Nature Reserve. Marram grass is the first plant to stabilize the sand, with its network of strong roots forming a rampart along the dunes. Behind its protection, sea holly, pink-flowered sea bindweed and the green-flowered sea spurge are found. A little further inland where there is a sandy soil, hawkweeds, brambles and restharrow grow. Where the sand is captured in the fixed dunes, burnet rose, orchids, ferns and lichens thrive, together with the Manx cabbage. The Manx cabbage, *Brassica Monensis,* was first discovered in 1662 by the botanist John Ray. It has a tall stem topped by a crown of yellow flowers, which turn to spreading seed pods as the summer progresses. Rare flowers flourish amongst the sand dunes,

uncommon orchids, lichens and ferns. Do not disturb them or gather their seeds. Some orchids do not produce seeds until about 14 years old. How tragic to trample on one that was 13$\frac{1}{2}$!

For a while the footpath uses an old railway trackbed, now colonized by flowers – lady's smock, red campion and various grasses. Many butterflies visit the area, the meadow brown, wall brown and orange tip. The bird's-foot trefoil is host to the common blue; the small copper likes to stay with the dock or sorrel; while the tall stinging nettles attract the peacock, tortoiseshell and red admiral. Other butterflies such as the large, small and grey-veined whites have moved in, so you are likely to see many caterpillars about. As you pass take care not to tread on them.

Birds

The island has its share of resident birds, but its position, roughly in the centre of the Irish Sea, also makes it an important staging post for many migrants. Binoculars are rewarding, and the footpaths give a grandstand view. An excellent comprehensive book, *Birds of the Isle of Man,* by J.P. Cullen & P. P. Jennings and beautifully illustrated by Alan Harris, will tell you every detail of the Manx birdlife. However, the following short summary may also be useful.

In the woodlands and glens the bigger birds, rooks, tree-nesting ravens and sparrowhawks, are easy to spot if they are about. The conifer plantations through which the Millennium Way and Bayr ny Skeddan pass have a population of tits, goldcrest, woodcock and the long-eared owl. I spent time by a plantation expecting to see these

Seagull

birds. I heard them, they were in good voice at about four o'clock in the morning, yet I saw only a black-headed gull and an owl.

On the upland moors and slopes of the mountains the curlew, snipe, skylark and meadow pipit try to steal the show, the red grouse and wheatear being less bold. I didn't see the hen harrier or the hooded crow, but a kestrel was having a dispute with a few herring gulls.

The thick stone and turf walls of the farmland, often crowned with gorse, ash or hawthorn, provide secret nesting sites for the robin, wren, pied wagtail, whitethroat and yellow hammer. As you walk through the fields in winter the visitors include fieldfare and redwing. In summer lapwing, golden plover and grey partridge are about. I got a nasty shock when a pheasant rose up under my nose with a frantic cry. These birds are very well camouflaged, as are the nests of ground-nesting birds, and appeals for care are often sited on the footpaths.

The Manx rivers are bright, busy streams, with grey wagtail, moorhens and mallard. Sad to tell, the dipper population has declined due to the pollution of some rivers by mining, but the good news is that the fish are returning, so perhaps the dippers will follow.

The coast provides two very different kinds of habitat. Where there are high cliffs the rocky ledges are occupied by colonies of seabirds. The dominant seabird is the herring gull, as the footpath waymark verifies, but there are other gulls and auks. Fulmar, kittiwake, guillemot, cormorant and shag all have their favourite ledges. Razorbill and puffin like to be close to the water, but the black-headed gull turns up everywhere.

The strip of land between the field edge and the cliff not only holds the footpath but is the territory of dunnock, robin, wren and stonechat. I had never seen the stonechat before I camped on the Raad ny Foillan. I heard a call, 'Tea, Jack, Jack', and on a gorse bush not a yard away was this lovely little bird. It has a black head, a white collar and a chestnut breast.

The sandy heaths of the Ayres are the nesting place of the little tern, the common tern, oystercatcher, ringed plover and curlew.

The greatest gathering of birds is on the intertidal mud flats, where each tide invites the waders to a banquet – oystercatchers, curlew, lapwing, golden plover, ringed plover, dunlin, sanderling, redshank – and the choughs, ducks and gulls join in too. Summer visitors can be seen resting and feeding. Sandwich terns, the red-breasted merganser and the Arctic skua have been recorded breeding on the island recently.

As you enjoy watching the birds, just appreciate that it is their habitat we are visiting and it has been our pleasure.

Grey Atlantic seal

Mammals

The Isle of Man has few native wild mammals, yet they well represent the different habitats to be found on or around the island.

Common and grey seals frequent the rocky inlets of the coast. The grey seal is often to be seen basking on the rocks. It is an inquisitive creature and is likely to follow you along the coast. I have been under its scrutiny many times as I walked the Raad ny Foillan. Basking sharks, huge but gentle, plankton-eating creatures, often play in the clear waters off Port Erin and the surrounding coast.

The pygmy shrew frequents the fields and hedgerows. Its Manx name, *Thollog Faiyr*, literally translated means 'the grass louse'. The stoat is common both in number and legend. If anyone kills a stoat it is said that revenge will soon follow.

There are three kinds of bat native to the island – the long eared, the natterers and the pipistrelle.

On the moors and mountains brown and mountain hares are often seen. The Manx name for the hare is *mwaag*.

The largest native wild mammal was the Irish 'elk', a giant deer now

27

extinct. It was a formidable creature standing 6 feet high with a 12 foot span of antlers. Skeletons of the elk found on the island are on exhibition in the Manx and Leeds museums. It is said that the animal's ghost can still be seen roaming the eastern glens.

The other animals on the island have been introduced, some so long ago that they have earned the right to be called Manx. The Loaghtan sheep was introduced from Scandinavia, its wool producing warm clothing in the times of the Vikings. The word *loaghtan* is a combination of two Manx words – *lugh*, meaning 'mouse' or 'sheep', and *dhone*, meaning 'brown'. It is a small agile breed, and a flock owned by the Manx National Heritage roam free on the clifftop pastures of Maughold Head. The Manx cat possesses only a tuft of hair where other cats have a tail. It was probably introduced from the mainland of Europe, where other tailless cats are known to occur.

The rabbit was introduced, but hedgehogs, mice and rats arrived by accident.

Of passing interest are the mainland animals which did not arrive. There are no badgers, foxes, moles or water rats. There are no snakes. Only the common and sand lizards represent the reptiles. No toads or newts are to be found, and it is only recently that frogs have become established.

The Isle of Man sadly has no squirrels, but perhaps, as the red squirrel is being so hard-pressed in the UK, a sanctuary may be offered one day.

The four-horned Loaghtan sheep

HISTORY

Today the lives of the Islanders are closely tied to the influence of their forefathers. Their way of life makes the Isle of Man unique, and its people justly proud of their rich heritage.

As I walked the Raad ny Foillan I was very much aware that I was walking hand in glove with history – seeing the same scenes Celtic eyes had seen, treading the same paths Pictish hunters had trod, resting on the same stones where Palaeolithic man once sat, and gazing out to sea as they had gazed. The Raad ny Foillan continually passes sites where much of Manx history occurred. There are remains of dwellings, magnificent castles, places

Neolithic stone circle, Mull Hill

of worship and graves of Manx forefathers. Many excellent books and booklets, written by notable authorities (see Appendix 2 for the Select Bibliography), recount the history of the island in detail. Below is a brief historical summary to enable the walker to recognise and appreciate the features along the coastline in the context of the island's history.

The earliest archaeological remains are of Palaeolithic (Old Stone Age) peoples dating from 2000 BC. They were hunters and gatherers using flint tools. Although many such tools have been found in Britain, only one has been found on Man, discovered in the soil of Rushen Abbey.

The next arrivals were the Neolithic Picts. They were a small, swarthy-skinned people, bold seafarers whose dwellings have been found on most coasts of Western Europe. Some settled in the Isle of Man, where they followed a prosperous lifestyle as herdsmen and farmers, exercising their bold spirits by raiding Roman Britain and earning the title of the dreaded 'Painted Men'.

The Picts lived in pit dwellings. A circular hole was dug in the ground and the earth from the pit piled around it. Suitable poles were anchored in the earth wall and sloped inwards to form a roof. Branches were woven between the poles and covered with a thatch of reeds leaving a smoke hole in the centre.

During the construction of Ronaldsway Airport a fine Pictish dwelling was discovered. Many artefacts, now in the Manx museum, led to the opinion that the family were 'farmers, happy, prosperous and well settled'. A stone axe found in the Ronaldsway dwelling was made at the Pike o' Stickle axe 'factory' in Langdale, in the English Lake District.

The Six Sheadings

Five stone plaques were also found at Ronaldsway, the like of which have not been discovered elsewhere in the British Isles. The largest one is oval, 3 inches long, as thin as a penny, and contains chevron and diamond patterns. Its use remains a mystery.

The Picts lived in groups or clans, the *bala* being the clan or family territory. The many place names beginning with Balla merely mean 'the farm of', followed by the owner's name or the name descriptive of the territory. As time passed the island became divided into a north and south territory – the north comprising the sheadings of Glenfaba, Michael and Ayre; the south those of Garff, Middle and Rushen. These Pictish names are still in use today.

The arrival of the Celts around 200 BC was a most important event in the island's history. The Celts arrived in Britain during the Bronze Age and,

being driven westward by other invaders from the continent of Europe, established themselves in Wales, Scotland, Ireland and the Isle of Man. In the Isle of Man they founded the language and the nation. The Manx language is closely related to Gaelic and is still spoken fluently by a few dedicated students. It is, however, in daily use in place names, family names, ceremony and song.

The Celts brought with them the skills and techniques of smelting iron. They built many forts on hills and promontories, which suggest that times were unsettled; the hill fort on South Barrule was the most important. The Celts drove the Picts into the more barren areas of the island, but in time they mingled to become one people.

Around the fifth century Christianity arrived with monks from Ireland. On the footpath the sites of many ancient *keeills* (churches) tell of the conversion of the island. One of these early saints was St Machud or Maughold who, it was said, died in AD 533 and was buried in Maughold churchyard. Scriptural scenes are depicted on some of the Celtic crosses in the collection at Maughold churchyard.

The Viking raiders first attacked Man in 798. The island became a 'Viking lair' from which attacks were launched on the neighbouring coasts. In 880 Harold Haarfager included Man in his Kingdom of the Southern Isles or Sudry, and united the Isle of Man politically.

King Orry, or Gorry, namely Godred Croven, after fighting against Harold at Stamford Bridge, conquered the Isle of Man. He established the Norse system of government as the national system, the Tynwald or Thingwald becoming the National Assembly *(thing – an assembly; vollr – a field)*. The Millennium of Tynwald was celebrated in 1979 by the introduction of the long-distance footpath across the island named the Millennium Way.

The history of the Manx nation continued to be troubled. In 1266 the island was sold to Scotland for 4000 marks, Alexander II becoming Lord of Man. In 1313 Bruce attacked and captured the Scandinavian stronghold on the site where Castle Rushen now stands. It was sold yet again in 1392 to William le Scrope. He was executed by Henry IV and the island was given to Henry Percy, Duke of Northumberland. There were changes still to come as the Percy's rebelled against Henry and in 1403 the island was given to John Stanley, 'in perpetuity', on the payment of homage and two falcons to him, and every future King of England, on his coronation day.

The Stanleys ruled as kings of Man for 350 years and a settled period of history began. Sir John Stanley, who was an absentee landlord and never visited the island, appointed a governor, who in turn appointed commissioners. On Lady Day 1423 a Tynwald court was summoned and the first Tynwald Manx 'Magna Carta' with written laws was recorded. So Tynwald and the House of Keys (the Scandinavian word *keise* meaning 'elected'), presided over by the Governor, dealt with the legislation of the island.

Queen Elizabeth II became Lord of Man in 1952. The island is still governed by its own parliament which meets, according to tradition, outdoors on July 5th, the Old Midsummer Day, on the Tynwald Hill at St John's. The foundation laid by the early settlers has moulded the island's way of life as you see it today and provided the means of legislation for the 1961 Rights of Way Act, the act which has completed the Raad ny Foillan for us to enjoy.

Celtic wheel cross at Maughold church

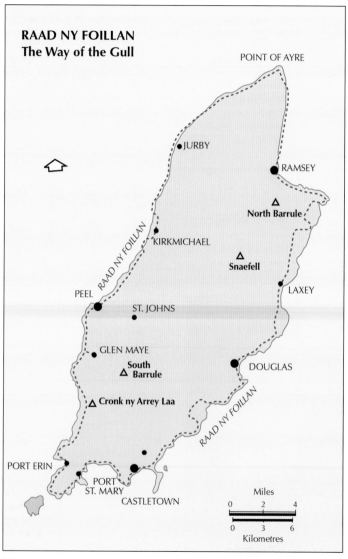

RAAD NY FOILLAN
The Way of the Gull

POINT OF AYRE

• JURBY

RAMSEY •

△
North Barrule

RAAD NY FOILLAN

KIRKMICHAEL

△
Snaefell

PEEL •

LAXEY

• ST. JOHNS

GLEN MAYE •

South
△ Barrule

DOUGLAS

△ Cronk ny Arrey Laa

RAAD NY FOILLAN

PORT ERIN •

•

PORT
ST. MARY
CASTLETOWN

Miles

0   2   4

0   3   6

Kilometres

RAAD NY FOILLAN:
The Way of the Gull

Ninety-eight miles

The Way of the Gull is officially 98 miles long, yet the route is very versatile. Sections can be done as single walks, each with their own unique character. Port St Mary to Port Erin is a superb walk, often with a fine sunset. Bradda Head, with an ascent of Milner's Tower, makes a gentle stroll. Rambling on Lhaittee ny Beinnee and Cronk ny Arrey Laa makes a fine mountain day. The Ayres Reserve offers peaceful picnic spots for nature lovers.

Douglas to Castletown

Distance:	15¾ miles
Maximum height:	300ft

At first glance a 3 mile walk round the Marine Drive may not be your idea of an unspoilt coastal path, but do not judge hastily. In a few minutes Douglas has dropped below and the Marine Drive is revealed as a road halfway up a 200ft cliff where man has failed to tame the elements. The tarmac, sprinkled by rocks from above and sprayed by the sea from below, holds a few motorists in search of 'a bit of fresh air' and the Raad ny Foillan footpath. The impressive facade is merely a hollow memorial to man's grand intentions to run a tramway. If you arrive on the overnight boat, the dawn over the sea, the rosy surf and the morning cry of the gulls will launch you on your way in worthy style.

The wide seascapes from the Marine Drive are rivalled by the position of this airy road, as it threads its

33

DOUGLAS

TOURIST INFORMATION
Isle of Man Department of Tourism and Leisure
Sea Terminal Building, Douglas, Isle of Man IM1 2RG
Tel: 01624 686766, Fax: 01624 627443, Website: www.visitisleofman.com
Leaflets available in English, French and German

ACCOMMODATION
See Tourist Information brochure; also list of B&B accommodation within easy reach of the coastal footpath.
Campsite: (May–Sept) Grandstand Campsite, Nobles Park, Douglas. Tel: 01624 842341 (during office hours)
    To reach the campsite from the quay, go along the Marine Drive. Pass the war memorial to the right then turn L up Broadway. Continue up Ballaquayle Road to traffic lights. Turn R signed to Ramsey. Just beyond the TT grandstand turn R, signed 'Police', then R into the campsite.

PUBLIC TRANSPORT
Service bus
Bus Station, Lord Street. Tel: 01624 663366 Douglas – Port Erin via Oatlands Lane End, Airport, Castletown and Port St. Mary; Douglas – Ramsay via Laxey; Douglas – Peel; Douglas – Ramsay via Peel and Kirk Michael; Town service via Nobles Park
Steam railway
Bank Hill Station. Tel: 01624 663366. All stations to Port Erin.
Manx electric railway
Tel: 01624 663366. Douglas to Ramsey via the coast. Numerous request stops.

SERVICES
Douglas – all amenities, hospital, sea terminal, sports complex.
Coastguard – Tel: 01624 661664
Port Soderick – Anchor Family Centre, open all year for drinks & refreshments, meals. Summer only

PLACES OF INTEREST
Manx Museum. Tel: 01624 648000, Crellin's Hill.

way across the formidable cliff face until the cliffs lower and Port Soderick is reached.

A shady glen leads inland from Port Soderick to a stretch of just over a mile on country lanes. Return to the coast is by the fields where the clifftop path is narrow, overgrown in places, but sound underfoot. The unspoilt coastline gives a feeling of remoteness. It is rocky with high cliffs and deep zawns. Spectacular views lie in every direction. After Cass-ny-Hawin the cliffs lower to shelving rocks and the walking becomes easier as the path widens.

At Derby Haven flocks of birds, feeding on the shallow bay, seem undisturbed by their noisy neighbours as they come into land at Ronaldsway Airport. A final road walk into Castletown gives you time to admire the situation of its fine castle.

Throughout the stage the views are excellent, gradually changing in the distance yet springing a sudden surprise near at hand. The path is firm but the cliff is under constant erosion from the prevailing south-west wind and weather, and the edge should only be approached with utmost caution.

Port Soderick

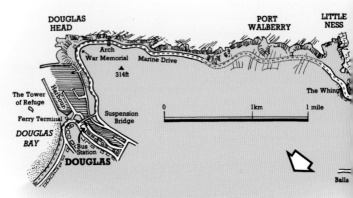

1. DOUGLAS to SANTON HEAD

The Route

Start at the swing bridge across the harbour in Bridge Street, where you will find the first waymark of the Raad ny Foillan. These signs, a white gull on a blue background, will guide you clockwise round the island and return you to this spot.

Cross the swing bridge and mount the flight of steps. Turn left along the road and proceed until the Manx Radio building is on the right. Take your first break here (seat) and look back because the views across Douglas Bay are magnificent.

Douglas is the capital of the island, its rise to prominence being mainly due to its deep-water harbour where the River Dhoo and the River Glass enter the sea. The underlying rock is shale, so the harbour is not a victim to silting, and with increasing trade the town has grown. The little isle in the bay is St Mary's Rock, with its tower

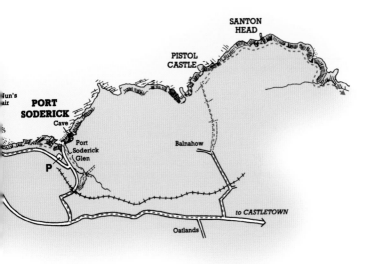

of refuge. Beyond the town the patchwork of fields merges into the distant moorland of Snaefell.

Continue along the road. At the first bend is the war memorial, then on the headland the scene changes. Go through a rock cutting where a concrete path leads left. A few yards along this stands the memorial stone presented to the island for help at the loss of the fishing boat *Solway Harvester* in January 2001, and a bird's-eye view of Douglas lighthouse.

The imposing turreted facade marks the entrance to the Marine Drive. Built in 1891 it presents an uneasy part-nership of brick and stone. The bracken- and heather-covered moorland ends in 200ft cliffs, which fall sheer in a deluge of crags, zawns, slides and pinnacles into the sea. The road threads its way across the face of this cliff.

The surfaced road has little traffic, so there is plenty of space for you to gaze seaward and enjoy views east-wards to Black Combe in the Lakeland hills. This is

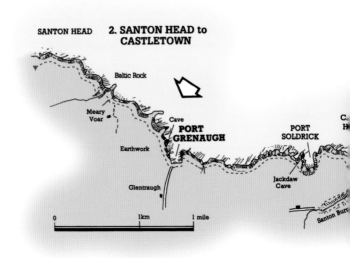

SANTON HEAD

2. SANTON HEAD to CASTLETOWN

Baltic Rock

Meary Voar

Cave

PORT GRENAUGH

Earthwork

PORT SOLDRICK

C. H

Glentraugh

Jackdaw Cave

Santon Burr

0   1km   1 mile

especially beautiful if you have landed from the overnight boat and dawn is creeping over the horizon.

Pass amazing rock scenery at The Whing, where earth movements have folded the rocks. Down the next deep zawn a detached rocky pinnacle can be seen at sea level. This is the Nun's Chair, where the naughty nuns from the Douglas Nunnery were put to do penance. The cliffs become lower. At the road junction turn left.

After ¼ mile look for a footpath which veers off to the left (w/m) and descends gently at first, then more steeply by zigzag steps, to the beach at Port Soderick. ◄

A walkway round the base of the cliffs ahead leads to a little cave. You can enter this and pop out through a cleft back on the walkway.

Pass the Anchor Family Centre using the beach and look for the waymark and signpost at the entrance to Port Soderick Glen.

Reverse Direction:
At the beach pass the Anchor Centre and turn left. Do not pass through the stone arch – this path leads to a fisherman's walkway – but search for a well-concealed flight of steps.

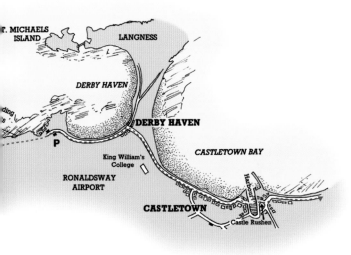

There are paths on either side of the stream, which meet and cross over little footbridges. A patch of open meadow, a lovely picnic spot, is passed. Carry on through the offset gap in a fence, keeping uphill and right on a bridle path to reach a lane.

Turn left. The lane goes under a railway bridge. Keep left again join a minor road (w/m). Turn left along the road, passing a small lake formed by a dam in the Crogga river.

Follow the road until opposite a terrace of cottages. The hill to the right behind the cottages is formed of Devonian granite – one of the few places where it appears on the surface. Just over the rise look for the waymark, which indicates a left turn into a narrower winding lane. Cross the railway bridge and climb the rise.

The railway you have just crossed is the steam railway from Douglas to Port Erin. You may have already heard a nostalgic whistle echoing over the fields, but this railway is very much alive. Gleaming engines gasping noisily pull their single-compartment coaches. The passengers, comfy in plush seats, use any excuse to let the window down by its leather strap.

The lane now bends towards a farm, but take the track to the right (w/m), leading to the fields, and scan the horizon for the next waymark. The track ends at a stile. Keep straight ahead through the fields, and as you reach the next waymark you will be rewarded with a magnificent view of the coastline. On the left are the crags of Pistol Castle, a fine array of cliffs enjoyed by birds and rock climbers. To the right is Santon Head where the next rock strata, the Agneash Grits, come to light.

Turn right along the shy footpath.

This narrow footpath between the cliff edge and the fence is almost hidden in the height of summer by gorse and bracken, yet it is sound underfoot. Open balconies of turf appear, and I found it idyllic to sit and enjoy the sight of the seabirds riding the air and skimming the cliff edge. Taking a break here made me feel this footpath really did belong to the gull. Sea thrift is abundant, as is the tiny scarlet pimpernel I found peeping from the foot of an old wall. Yellow and blue pimpernel also grow, but I have still to find them.

Baltic Rock with Stanton Head behind

Jackdaw Cave at Port Soldrick

Continue along the footpath, which winds over Santon Head, crossing the stream near Baltic Rock by a footbridge. The protruding, yet easily accessible Baltic Rock gives fine coastal views. Cross a footbridge at Purt Veg. After passing a large telephone cable sign follow the stone wall, and there is a waymark by a stile which leads down into Grenaugh Cove. Before you descend into the cove look around.

Here was the Viking fortified farm of Cronk-ny-Merrieu, protected on the seaward side by the cliff and on the landward side by a rampart with a fosse (ditch). The building was late 11th century, yet when the site was excavated in 1950 traces of Iron Age occupation were found. Port Grenaugh is Scandinavian for 'sunny harbour'.

The lane gives access to the road and telephone (1 mile).

Leave the bay by crossing a bridge. The path slants upwards to gain the cliff edge again on the opposite side of the cove. From here to Port Soldrick the path lies between the cliff edge and the field, but in places it can be overgrown.

The path continues until a squat cove, Port Soldrick, is reached. Here the path divides, allowing you to choose your route. You can either skirt the cove by a

Aeroplane coming in to land at Ronaldsway

King William's College, Castletown

circle of the cove rim along an indistinct path, much overgrown, or make a descent into the cove.

The descent is better. When level with the beach continue straight ahead by a path up the other side cut through a tunnel of vegetation. On reaching the cliff top a fine sea cave on the east side of the cove can be seen and the views are splendid back to Santon Head and forward to Langness and Castletown.

Caves on the coastline bring to mind smugglers, and this is Jackdaw Cave, a genuine smugglers' hideout. Boats entered the cave and were secretly loaded through a hole in the roof. Around the year 1700 the island was being used as a 'trading' centre for brandy. Manx merchants would buy brandy and silks from France and rum from Jamaica. The goods were then brought to the Isle of Man duty free in the fast Manx clippers. This was quite legal. The same clippers then ran cargoes to quiet coves on the Welsh, Cheshire, Lancashire, Scottish and Irish coasts.

The Manx were skilful sailors, knowing every inch of the Irish Sea, and the British revenue cutters were continually outmanoeuvred. The smugglers have gone and so have the jackdaws. Housemartins are the present tenants.

In a short while you will pass Cass-ny-Hawin Head and approach the deep inlet of Cass-ny-Hawin, where

43

*Harbour light,
Castletown*

the Santon Burn enters the sea. Across the inlet the rocky knoll with sea caves at its foot and an earthwork on top is your objective.

A decision has to be made here. If the tide is out and the Santon Burn is not in flood it is possible to easily cross the stream. The best descent is by a steep path about 20yds past the signpost. After crossing the stream near the gorge entrance either take an exposed, crumbling path up the steep hillside above, or (safer) go left along the beach below a rock headland to a much easier path. If you cannot take the shortcut then you must make a detour upstream along the official path. It takes to a field on the right for a short way, then a w/m points the way back left into the bushes and trees above the stream. Eventually cross a stile to gain a bridge over Santon Burn. Turn left downstream, go through a gate (w/m) and continue through the bushes to reach a sunken track with a wall on the left. Climb to a signpost at its head and turn left to emerge eventually in the meadows near Cass-ny-Hawin earthworks and a junction with the shortcut. Keep on the seaward side of the meadow on a pleasant grassy path as the cliffs lower.

The quarry on your right announces a change of rock to the Carboniferous limestone. It is a working quarry, the rock being used for roadstone. ▸ Pass by the gantry, which holds the landing lights for Ronaldsway Airport. Across the shallow bay of Derby Haven, St Michael's Island attracts the eye.

The island is joined to Langness by a causeway, and the ruin of St Michael's Chapel stands a silhouette against the sea. The chapel was built on the site of an ancient Celtic keeill, *the round fort being erected about 1540. The tall tower on Langness (1800) is impressive but its original purpose remains uncertain; a watchtower against the fleet of Napoleon or a beacon tower is the most popular theory. If the tide is on the turn, Derby Haven becomes a birdwatchers' paradise as all the seabirds in the area are attracted to feast. To be seen are: duck, curlew, plover, dunlin, lapwing, redshank, widgeon, snipe and curlew sandpiper. In winter bar-tailed godwit and choughs congregate.*

At Derby Haven turn right at the telephone box.

The narrow neck of land between Derby Haven and Castletown Bay is Ronaldswath or Ronald's Way. Boats were hauled across the isthmus to avoid the difficult tide race round Langness. King Ronald laid a paved way to make the task easier. Langness Light on Dreswick Point, one of the four Manx lighthouses, guards this section of the coast.

On the right the buildings of King William's College demand your attention. A fund begun by Bishop Barrow in the 17th century provided grants for deserving pupils, and in 1830 a general appeal by the Governor to add to these funds resulted in the building of this well-known public school; King William IV was approached for a donation, but as he had no money at the time he gave it his name instead! The new building was unfortunately destroyed by fire in 1844 with the loss of many valuable documents. Public subscription was again generous and the fine building of local limestone is the one you see today.

Follow the road round the bay and along the harbour into Castletown. Cross the swing bridge (for toilets go over road bridge on right) to the town centre. Tap on quay opposite harbour office.

Diversion

An extension of the Ronaldsway Airport runway has temporarily closed the footpath. At the quarry turn R, then at the next T junction L to follow the A12 along the perimeter of the airport towards Ballasalla until meeting the A5.* This road is busy leading past the airport entrance to meet the footpath again on the coast by King William's College near Castletown.

* Alternatively, at the A5/A12 junction go ahead and over the railway into Ballasalla. At the second roundabout bear left to Rushen Abbey and follow the Herring Way, Bayr ny Skeddan (see page 148), to Castletown.

Castletown to Port St Mary

Distance:	6¾ miles
Maximum height:	sea level

A very easy and fast section. Road walking gives way to
a track with views back to Castletown, Derby Haven and
Langness Point. From Scarlett Point a smooth grassy path
is on gently shelving turf along the low rocky shoreline.
This is part of the Scarlett Nature Trail.

The extensive seascape panoramas are captivating
and continually changing. The coast from Langness to
Spanish Head and the Calf of Man is on view. There is a
stretch of road walking from Poyllvaaish to Rhenwyllan,
then a good footpath and the firm sand of Chapel Bay
lead to Port St Mary.

*Castletown harbour
is dominated by
Castle Rushen*

CASTLETOWN

TOURIST INFORMATION
Town Hall, Parliament Square. Tel: 01624 825005
Information Office in the Old Grammar School (between the Square and the harbour parking).

ACCOMMODATION
See list

PUBLIC TRANSPORT
Bus
Castletown – Airport, Douglas, Port St Mary, Port Erin, Peel
Steam Train
Stations to Douglas, Port Erin

SERVICES
Full range of shops. Market Day – Thursday morning (summer only)
Swimming Pool

PLACES OF INTEREST
Castle Rushen, The Nautical Museum, the original House of Keys, Scarlett Nature Trail & Visitor Centre

The Route

The focal point of Castletown is the market square. Its historic charm is renowned as a film setting, and in 2003 electric streetlights were replaced by gas lamps and antique bicycles, brooms and wheelbarrows prepared for the filming of *Five Children and It*. Leave the square by the south-west corner. The road soon divides, and on a 'no through road' signpost the Raad ny Foillan waymark will be seen.

The coast road is then followed. On the shore there are more birds to be seen. Look for herons, almost invisible, patiently fishing. There may be other waders and the goldeneye – a neat little black-and-white duck, the male having a black-green head, the female a chestnut; they look as though they are wearing a woolly balaclava.

47

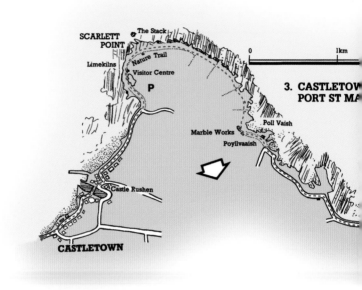

The coast road soon turns left to a track along the edge of the bay towards Scarlett Point.

The water-filled quarry on your right was once a major industry. Limestone for building was loaded into ships from the jetty, the remains of which are on your left. The quarry closed at the end of the 19th century after supplying stone for the southern branch of the Isle of Man Railway. As you pass the quarry, spare a moment to look at the fine view of Castletown. Opposite the southern end of the quarry, at sea level, are three limekilns. It is well worth the scramble down the slope to view these. Take care, they are being eroded and recent stonefalls have taken place. The small isolated building was the gunpowder store.

Back on the path is the Scarlett Visitor Centre. There is a nature trail round Scarlett Point – in fact you have

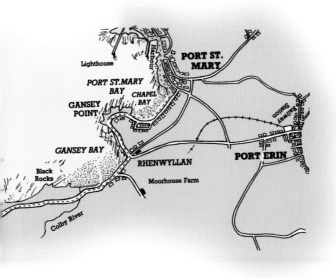

already walked some of it. *The small booklet published by the Manx Conservation Trust is full of information and is excellent value. It is available from the centre or from the local Information Office.*

Just beyond the gunpowder store the limestone slabs were split and intruded to give a dolerite dyke. This is now being eroded by the sea. The path passes the old lighthouse. Limestone-loving flowers grow. Those willing to tolerate the salty atmosphere – thyme, sea thrift, bird's-foot trefoil, stonecrop and sea spurrey – can be seen. As you progress along the rocky shore views open to the west. On a clear day you can see the old Chicken Rock Lighthouse 6½ miles away and the Burroo Rock, the large rock with the natural arch off the southern tip of the Calf of Man.

As Port St Mary and Spanish Head come into sight a stile and a waymark confirm the way.

Castletown from Scarlett Point

Scarlett Point takes its name from Skarfakluft, the Norse word meaning 'cormorant's cleft'. The most southerly rock of the point is the Stack, its basalt ledges being a favourite perch for cormorants, shags, auks and gulls.

Scarlett Point was also one of the 'Day Watch Hills'. Documents from the Scandinavian period of 1627 tell of the duty of Ward and Watch. Men were obliged to report from sunrise to sunset 'For serious duty and properly armed'.

Continue along the path, perhaps making brief excursions to examine the lichens which grow on the rocks (see section on Plants, p.23). Poyll Vaaish Quarry and its workshop are soon passed on the right. Poyll Vaaish means 'Bay of Death', said to be due to the black marble of the sea bed.

The limestone of this quarry has been meta-morphosed (heated by volcanic contact) three times. Today it is cut and polished for fancy goods and paving stones. Stone steps of Poyll Vaaish marble were the island's contribution to the building of St Paul's Cathedral. When the steps became worn they were retired to an upstairs gallery.

After passing the workshop the path changes to a track. Ignore a signpost showing a footpath returning to Castletown over the fields. Go straight on through the farmyard and onto the road (w/m). This road soon joins the main road from Castletown to Port St Mary. Turn left towards Port St Mary (w/m). A section of road-walking is now necessary, but it is not as tedious as may be suspected. The pavement is on the seaward side, and extensive views and, perchance, a performance of water

The old limekiln, Scarlett Point

A raised walkway leads to Port St Mary

skiers enhance the plod. At the pub where the Colby road turns right a major fault line changes the strata and the Barrule slates appear once more.

Continue past the road branching right to Port Erin, and at Rhenwyllan look for a waymark where the footpath turns left. The footpath passes by a group of pretty cottages, then after rounding the point you can choose to walk along the beach or on the pavement round Chapel Bay to Port St Mary. The town clings to the hillside and a flight of steps leads up through gardens to the town. To continue the Raad ny Foillan stay at sea level, and after passing through the gardens a raised walkway leads past cottages to the picturesque harbour.

Port St Mary to Port Erin

Distance:	7 miles
Maximum height:	400ft

This section of the Raad ny Foillan is a whisket of pleasure, from which I sample memories by the fireside on long winter evenings.

From the map it may appear to be just a quick 2 hour stroll, but it is a section on which to linger. After leaving Port St Mary the way passes Kallow Point then, rising round Perwick Bay, joins a quiet lane. The lane rises steeply, then is left behind as you enter the Manx National Trust area for Public Ramblage, The Chasms. The footpath circles high above The Chasms and Bay Stacka, where the views are breathtaking. The footpath is sound and clearly marked. The grass changes to moorland, and the path narrows as it passes Black Head and

Port St Mary harbour

PORT ST MARY

TOURIST INFORMATION
Town Hall, Promenade. Tel: 01624 832101

ACCOMMODATION
B&B
Wide choice – see list and Tourist Information brochure

PUBLIC TRANSPORT
Bus
Port Erin, Castletown, Douglas, Peel
Service to Sound in school holidays
Buses run from the harbour
Trains
Stations to Douglas, Port Erin

SERVICES
Full range of shops
Early closing Thursday

PLACES OF INTEREST
Cregneish Village Folk Museum.
Open early May – late September, weekdays and Sunday afternoons.
Mull Hill stone circle

Spanish Head. The Calf of Man and its Sound dominate
the view to the west. The Calf Sound and its treacherous
tide race draws many sightseers, but their presence
warrants a cafe and toilets and a limited bus service.
There are no dogs allowed from here to Port Erin (see
alternative route via Mull Hill, below). The footpath then
takes a rising traverse, passing Aldrick and continuing
onto the open moor high above Bay Fine, until a descent
is made into the sheltered bay of Port Erin.

A worthwhile excursion can be made to Cregneish,
a traditional Manx village maintained as a folk museum,
and the Mull Hill Circle, a Neolithic monument unique
in Britain in its fine state of preservation.

Dramatic cliffs overlook The Sugarloaf

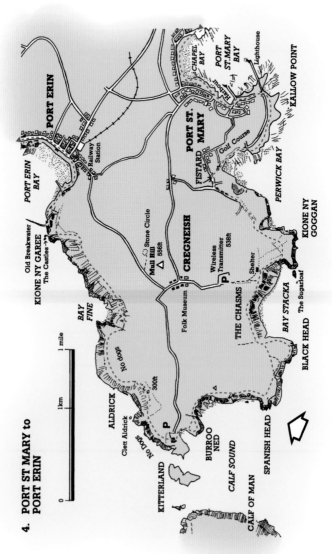

4. PORT ST MARY to PORT ERIN

The Route

To continue the Raad ny Foillan turn left from the way-mark at the south-west corner of the harbour (toilets) and stroll along the side of the harbour, sampling its nautical flavour and sea-borne smells. Turn right to walk along between the Island Seafood factories.

The Island Seafood is an expanding industry export-ing fresh white fish, smoked salmon, kippers, lobsters, scallops and queenies to the UK and Europe. A factory shop sells the products locally, and seafood can be ordered through the website at <u>www.islandseafare.co.uk</u>. Scallops are bivalves. They swim about by flap-ping strong valves attached to their two pink-and-white ribbed shells. It is whilst they are swimming that they are caught by the local fishermen. As one sailor in springtime bemoaned as he mended his nets, 'Catches are bad. The sea hasn't warmed up yet and the queenies are all in bed'. The waters of the Irish Sea are monitored by the Marine Laboratory, Port Erin, and the quality of the water is steadily improving.

Pass the lifeboat station and find a waymark, where you can stay on the road or use the footpath along the sea wall to Kallow Point. Here you can enjoy the expanding views eastwards to Langness Point and west-wards to The Chasms. Pass a colonnaded shelter, then as the footpath nears the road move once more onto it and continue on a track ahead (w/m). A post stile gives access to a concrete path, which mounts between the golf course and the edge of the now heightening cliffs. Do not take the small path on the left – this leads down to the shore – but keep on the paved path. A gate gives onto the road at a private housing development. Follow waymark signs into an enclosed pathway between high hedges to a kissing gate (w/m). This opens onto a narrow lane. Turn left down the lane and cross Glenchass Bridge. Ignore the lane left and continue up the hill, where a fingerpost signs you to The Chasms.

As the gradient eases the views unfold. At a junction keep straight on (w/m). The path is now along a walled track opening into a pasture. You are now in the National

The old café, now a shelter, above The Chasms

Trust area of Public Ramblage. Please observe the countryside code and leave this wild and beautiful area as you discovered it. Over the cliff edge is Kione-y Ghoggan (The Anvil), a favourite breeding spot for guillemots, kittiwakes and puffins.

The exit to the field is right to a gate. Next make your way diagonally left almost to the point where the fence guards the dizzy edge of The Chasms.

Many seabirds nest on the cliffs – guillemots, razorbills, fulmars, petrels, shags and kittiwakes. Choughs like the security of The Chasms' cracks for their nests, and ravens are regular visitors. Directly below lies the Sugarloaf, the island's finest sea stack. It was first climbed in 1933 by Dr. A.W. Kelly, one of the pioneer rock climbers on the island. He approached by boat and climbed the stack alone. There have been few subsequent ascents, for the rock is both loose and lubricated with bird droppings.

The Chasms are great rifts in the earth caused by severe earth movements. They vary in width from a few inches to several feet; in depth they split the rocks to below sea level. The fissures are overgrown with heather and other vegetation, and there have been accidents. So be safe – stay on the path.

Go uphill to an old building. This building is the former Chasms cafe (Excursion to Cregneish and Mull Hill (see box) starts from this point). It may not look attractive, but it has a seat and provides shelter. From the climbers' gate in the wall below the shelter is a view of the Sugar Loaf and The Chasms, which becomes more dramatic if you advance a little toward the cliff edge.

On leaving the shelter continue by the clifftop wall to a stile – National Trust sign. Over the stile the path threads its way through the heath. To the right the automatic-wireless transmitting direction-finding station can be seen. Ignore the stile leading right, signpost and continue descending the narrow path. Cross a small stream soon then climb up over Black Head onto Spanish Head. The main path forks left over the shoulder to gain the edge and

Excursion to Cregneish and Mull Hill

From the old Chasms cafe the path leads uphill towards a car park at the radio beacon. Go through the car park and straight along the narrow lane to the old Manx village of Cregneish. The thatched cottages have been pre-served and furnished by the Manx Museum and National Trust as a folk museum. You can obtain a ticket from Cullan Beg, one of the more modern houses, which will entitle you to an enlightening chat in the various cot-tages. If closed it is still worth walking round the village and peeping in the windows.

To visit the Mull Hill Stone Circle, take the uphill road through the village to the main road. At the main road leading to the Sound turn left, then take the next fork right along the minor road signed 'Port Erin'. On the right just beyond a stony track, a path slants up the hillside. At the top of the hill is the stone circle of Mull Hill.

The Meayll or Mull Circle is a Neolithic monument unique in Great Britain. Its ancient name is Rhullick-y-lag-sliggagh or 'the graveyard of broken slates'. This is a remarkable late Neolithic burial ground situated just below the ruins of Pictish villages. Originally it was a round barrow containing six sets of graves, each set consisting of three stone chambers arranged in a 50ft-diameter circle. Urns containing human ashes, flint heads, scrapers, knives and small pottery vessels which had once contained food were found inside. C.W. Airne, in his book The Story of the Isle of Man, *poses the question 'Why did the Picts who grew wheat on Mull Hill cremate their dead and bury their ashes in a round barrow?' One thing we do know, they chose a wonderful viewpoint.*

Late Neolithic burial chamber, Mull Hill

amazing views of the cliffs. The Chicken Rock Lighthouse and the Calf of Man are can be seen over the Sound.

Why Chicken Rock? A quote from Kingsley's The Water Babies *and you will have an answer. 'There came by a flock of petrels who said, "We are Mother Carey's own chickens, she sends us out all over the seas to show the good birds the way home"'. The stormy petrels still come home to the Calf of Man. The name Mother Carey dates back to pre-Reformation England and came from the Latin Mater Cara, meaning 'dear mother'. Mother Carey's chickens were, in legend, sent to warn sailors of approaching storm and it was considered very unlucky to kill them. 'Petrel' is said to come from the Italian 'Petrelo' or 'Little Peter' because the birds appear to walk on the water as they fly low with their feet dangling on the water surface.*

Spanish Head

Bay Stacka with the Sugarloaf

The path now goes along the cliff top then descends to cross a small ghyll. Tourists take a shortcut from here across the field to the car park, but if you turn left after crossing the ghyll a fingerpost directs the way clockwise round the knoll, where you will be rewarded by a prime viewpoint over the Sound. Continue past the memorial to Sir Percy Cowley, a Manxman who unlocked the gate leading to the open countryside we now enjoy. Signpost. Arrive at the Sound Cafe (car park and toilets, bus terminus).

The Calf of Man is separated from its parent by the Sound and is now a National Trust area open for Public Ramblage. There is a bird observatory which offers day facilities and accommodation to the birdwatcher. Daily visits are arranged from Port Erin, and those who wish to stay longer can apply to the Isle of Man Department of Tourism and Leisure for details. Many birds nest there, but alas it has been almost abandoned by the Manx shearwater. In 1786 rats escaped from the wreck of a Russian ship. They attacked the helpless fledglings and the colony was abandoned by the birds. They have rarely been seen since.

The Sound, with the Calf of Man on the left

Other tales of woe were attached to the Calf. The Chicken Rock Lighthouse was badly damaged by fire in 1960. It now houses an automatic light and fog signal.

Many ships have come to grief in the Sound. The passage is encumbered with rocks and tidal currents running at 3–3$^1/_2$ knots, resulting in overfalls and eddies. I once had the pleasure of looking round a naval survey vessel and was shown an underwater chart of the Sound of Man. It looked like a grand canyon with pinnacles of jagged rock, caves, holes and fissures. Spectacular to see, but needing the skill of 'Manannan Mac Lir, a celebrated merchant of the Isle of Man, who was the best pilot living in Western Europe' to navigate. So says an ancient Irish manuscript of AD 900.

To the north of the cafe is the Thousla Cross. It stands in memory of the local men who lost their lives in the rescue of the crew of the French schooner *Jeane St Charles* in 1858. Pass the Thousla Cross below the cafe. ◄

A stile gives access to open grassy slopes (w/m and fingerpost). The path climbs the grass slope to a green balcony. Look up leftwards above a collection of boulders to the horizon, where a fingerpost can be seen. The path rises and another fingerpost comes into view as you gain height. The path then curves leftwards along the green balcony and passes through the boulders to reach a stile by the fingerpost that you spotted on the horizon. The footpath has gained the 200ft contour. Far below are the crags of Bay Fine, the breeding place for a colony of black guillemots. The path wanders between the fence and the cliff top, its position giving views of the Calf of Man. If the tide race is in full flow you will hear why it is called 'The Sound'. Bradda Head with the Milner Tower now dominate the scene to the north.

Another stile and fingerpost are passed, and an assortment of rising sheep tracks on the open moor lead to another fingerpost. Continue on a rising path until, as you round the shoulder of the moor, Port Erin comes into view. The path now descends gently, bending right as it

No dogs are allowed beyond this point (see alternative route, next page).

Port Erin Bay and Bradda Head

Alternative route (dogs permitted)
From the stile (see page 64) walk up the road, which gives good retrospective views. Turn left signed Port Erin to pass Mull Hill stone circle on the right. Follow this road to Port Erin.

follows a wall. A wire fence bars the way, but there is a gate at its seaward end. The path hugs the fence then turns sharp right through a gate (fingerpost). A sheltered pathway between fence and wall leads to Port Erin. Over the wall is the favourite gossiping spot of the Port Erin gulls, and you have the chance to study them here at very close quarters. This is indeed the way of the gull.

Descend to the harbour by a flight of steps on the left. The building on your left is the Marine Biological Interpretation Centre run by Liverpool University.

Boat trips to the Calf of Man leave daily from the harbour (weather permitting). These are working boats. If you take a trip you may return accompanied by lobsters and richer for the interesting conversation with the Port Erin fishermen.

The road past the harbour leads to the promenade telephone box by the beach where the next section starts.

Port Erin to Peel

Distance:	14½ miles
Maximum height:	1434ft

This is a mountain section over the Carnanes with three summits, Bradda Hill, Lhiattee ny Beinee and Cronk ny Arrey Laa, each one higher, wilder and more remote than its predecessor. The western side of each hill plunges in sheer cliffs to the sea giving views to which I cannot do justice. If the visibility is poor, serious thought should be given to using the lower level alternative way to the east (see map pages 70–71 and 78–79). Map and compass are essential.

The road walk along the promenade, although short and attractive, can be further improved by taking the traversing path part-way down the cliff. You are soon onto open pastures, which change to wild moorland.

Port Erin

PORT ERIN

TOURIST INFORMATION
Commissioner's Office, Station Road. Tel: 01624 832298

ACCOMMODATION
B&B
Port Erin – See Tourist Information brochure

PUBLIC TRANSPORT
Bus Depot
Port Erin – Douglas via Port St Mary, Castletown, Airport. Port Erin – Peel via
Castletown. Airport, Ballasalla, Foxdale, St Johns – Cregneish
Steam Trains
Stations to Douglas. Daily except Saturday.

SERVICES
Full range of shops. Early closing Thursday.

PLACES OF INTEREST
Marine Biological Interpretation Centre. Boat trips round the Calf of Man.
Birdwatching visits to the Calf of Man. Steam Railway Museum.

Superb views unfold as height is gained to the Milner
Tower. The traverse over Bradda Hill is on good paths,
yet wild and magnificent, ending in a steep descent to
Fleshwick Bay.

The ascent of Lhiattee ny Beinee rises steeply from
Fleshwick Bay. On leaving the intake wall the way is
across moorland paths on the seaward side of a broad
ridge where the atmosphere is wild and the views excit-
ing. A steep descent is made to The Sloc, where the road
is approached.

The ascent of Cronk ny Arrey Laa (1434ft) is on a
well-trodden path. This is the highest point reached by
the Raad ny Foillan. On the descent to Niarbyl magnificent panoramas lie in every direction. A section of road
(1 mile) is followed by a return to the coast. A short visit
to Glen Maye leads to coastal meadowland until the

traverse round Corrin's Hill and onto Peel Hill brings the grand finale, the sudden display of St Patrick's Isle with its ancient castle.

The Route

By the telephone box on the lower promenade is a millennium commemorative paved area with seats, its sea wall illustrating with ingenuity the history of Port Erin. From this point as you face the sea turn right and make your decision. For the recommended alternative route see page 70. The official way takes the upper promenade until you see the waymark on your left. A gate opens onto a green path sandwiched between a wall and a fence. This path is soon joined from the left by the Coronation Footpath to Bradda Head. At this point the alternative way from Port Erin (see below) meets the Raad ny Foillan.

Turn left by the wall along the green path, which gradually gains height, the view improving with every step. The path widens then swings back left until the last steeper climb takes you to the doorway of the Milner Tower. You can climb the spiral staircase to the viewing platform.

Port Erin beach

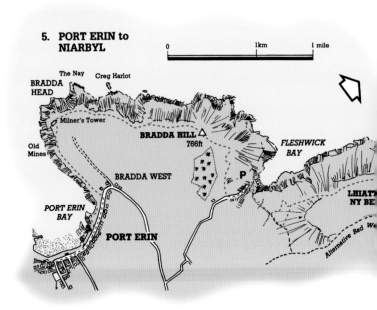

5. PORT ERIN to NIARBYL

0   1km   1 mile

The Nay   Creg Harlot
BRADDA
HEAD

Milner's Tower

BRADDA HILL △
766ft

FLESHWICK
BAY

Old
Mines

BRADDA WEST

P

LHIAT
NY BE

PORT ERIN
BAY

Alternative Bad We

PORT ERIN

Alternative route from Port Erin

From the telephone box walk a few yards north along the beach where the freshwater spring of St Catherine's Well issues. It was this spring which first attracted seafarers to this sheltered bay. Go up the steps at the well and turn left along the lower promenade, between the houses and their seaside gardens. Fuchsia grows in profusion and is one of the pleasures of a summer visit. A longer flight of steps takes you to the level of the upper promenade. Do not walk far along the pavement but take to the lawns on its left, where a paved walkway begins. You follow this walkway left as it threads its way along the face of the vegetated cliff. Continue past the old swimming pool, a relic of the past. Do not take an upward way to the road but keep traversing the cliff path round the next cove. You will soon arrive at the Bradda Glen cafe. Walk straight on through the grounds. This viewpoint over the bay is a

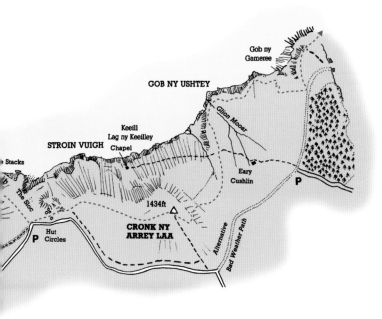

place to see basking sharks. After the cafe a signpost 'Coronation Footpath' points to the right. Follow this path through a gap in the wall and you are on the Raad ny Foillan again.

St Catherine's Well, Port Erin

Milner's Tower is a fine viewpoint

William Milner was a Liverpool safe maker. About the year 1864 he was active in the erection of a breakwater to shelter the bay from the westerly winds and make a harbour of refuge for the fishermen. When the foundation stone was laid he threw a great party for the whole neighbourhood. In gratitude and respect for their benefactor the tower was built during his lifetime. It was built in the shape of one of his earlier keys.

If you look away across the sea to the south you may see the legendary Manannin Isle. This isle, it is said, rises above the waves on Midsummer Day every seventh year. A strange boat brings an assortment of enchanted fairy folk to Port Erin. Do not get entangled with them, or you will have to accompany them to their watery home under the sea. There you will have to work for the Sea King until Midsummer Day seven years hence.

From the tower descend the way you came for 100yds, passing the spot where the world's winning photograph was taken (see plaque on tower). Next pass an old mine building, and continue on the right of the fence and spoil heaps. If you scratch around, pieces of pyrite (fool's gold) can be found. Copper, lead and silver were mined here until about 1880. The path now follows the cliff top, gaining height towards Bradda Hill. As the path rises and the height above the sea increases you are

Impressive cliff scenery from the Bradda mines

Note: It would be an advantage at this spot to survey the route ahead. Look for the point where the intake wall from Fleshwick Bay turns a right angle south and the Raad ny Foillan goes ahead to another wall corner up the ridge of Lhiattee ny Beinee.

treated to dramatic glimpses of the surf far below. The grass gives way to bracken and heather as the path climbs in two stages to its highest point. From here a small track on the right leads to the summit cairn at 726ft. The path now heads in an easterly direction towards Fleshwick Bay. Cross the wall at the Public Right of Way sign. ◀

Descend the steep zigzag path down the bracken slopes between the plantation and the coast (a minor crag is avoided by one of the descending traverses of the path). A gate leads into a field. Cross the field to the road (w/m). Turn left down the road to the beach.

Fleshwick Bay, derived from the Scandinavian 'fles-vik' or 'green creek', is a favourite haunt of scuba divers. The surrounding cliffs turn this little bay into a suntrap and the clear water made me want to take a dip myself. I quickly changed my mind when wet-suited divers emerged saying they would come back later in the year when the water had warmed up!

The waymark on the fingerpost by the beach invites you to jump across the stream and set off up the rough grass-covered slope towards a beckoning second fingerpost. The path crosses the head of a deep-cut zawn. At the second fingerpost you encounter a boggy area. Squelch across to a fingerpost and stile. Gain the side of the wall. Follow the smooth dry path now running parallel to the stone wall just left of dense bracken until the wall turns off to the right at a corner. You can either continue ahead to the topmost corner of the next wall and turn left on a traversing path, or go the following shorter way.

Gain an isolated signpost in the moor on the left, and turn left here to reach another sign. Go left again along an old track towards a low crag. Bend right just before it and climb to join the horizontal path of the other way. Turn left onto the broad gentle ridge, where the way becomes more distinct. A previously unseen, sea-washed aspect of Bradda Head comes into view. At the highest point of the cliff you can take a break and, if the visibility is good, identify the Mountains of Mourne on the western horizon.

In September this moor is a carpet of colour. The purple of the heather mixed with the bright yellow of the late-summer-flowering short gorse is a sight to see, mingled here and there with patches of white cotton grass (not really a grass but a sedge).

Pass a cairn and keep on the edge overlooking the coast. Cross the remains of an old wall.

A brief excursion nearer the edge will enable you to sample a new panorama north. Extending into the sea is the rock spit of Niarbyl (the tail of the rocks), and beyond it Corrin's Hill, near Peel, can be seen.

Continue along the path to the large cairn on the summit of Lhiattee ny Beinee, 988ft.

From the cairn view the panorama. Circling from east to west you can see the Manx radio mast at Douglas, the south-east coast, Ronaldsway, the Langness Peninsula, Scarlett Point, the Calf of Man and Bradda Head. On a very clear day it is possible to see the Lancashire hills to the east, the Irish mountains to the west and, peeping over the southern horizon, the Welsh mountains.

The path follows the broad ridge. This soon steepens and descends through the heather to a waymark on a signpost at The Sloc, the gap between the two hills. The

Cronk ny Arrey Laa from Lhiattee ny Beinee

main path goes straight to the road, car park and picnic area. (The waymarked route, now a mere trod, goes ahead to the wall and stile, then turns right to the roadside.)

Alternative bad-weather route

The path to the west of the road skirts the foot of the mountain, then climbs gradually to meet the road on the col between Cronk ny Arrey Laa and North Barrule. Turn left along the road then left again onto a track. Follow this downhill to a parking area at a corner of the Kerroodhoo Plantation. Keep straight on and meet the Raad ny Foillan again at the Gob ny Gameree viewpoint near Cregganmoar (see below).

Begin the ascent of Cronk ny Arrey Laa on the path between the crag and the road. Go through a gap in the fence. The wall now bends right following the road with North Barrule to the east. Our path goes straight on. A path forks right. This is the bad-weather route (see below), kept clear of heather by off-road bikers.

Keep an eye on the crown of the small hill to the left as you now take a rigid line for the summit of Cronk ny Arrey Laa. When you have gained a few hundred feet turn and look back.

The flat top of the small hill now reveals an ancient earthwork, the site of a Pictish village where Neolithic farmers tilled the land. They feared tribal raids when times were hard and built a stronghold on the crown of the hill, surrounded by a ditch with pointed stakes and hurling stones. Little of this remains, but the outlines of their pit dwellings, the walls being built of stone slabs, can clearly be seen today.

The path is steep and the name of the hill, Cronk ny Arrey Laa (Hill of the Morning Watch), gives food for thought until you notice a sudden change of gradient. Keep straight on up the moorland to reach the huge summit cairn at 1434ft.

This is no ordinary cairn but a prehistoric burial mound, probably of the early Bronze Age, about

*Cronk ny Arrey
Laa summit cairn*

1500 BC. It has been excavated, and its summit was restored in 1958. Cronk ny Arrey Laa was a Watch hill, as were the other hills on the western side of the island. The watchman in his position of trust could look out as you can now, over the southern half of Man, spread at his feet. Papers in Castle Rushen dated 1627 set out the punishments for failure to report and for going to sleep on duty. For the first duty failed the watchman must 'Forfiet bodye and goodes'. For the second failure the 'forfiet' was 'a cowe'. The third time involved surrender of 'Lyfe and Lyme to yr Lorde' – which sounds nasty. It was the poor widows I felt sorry for. Because of the wind the 'widdows' of the island had to 'gather fuel for fires for warmth and the beacon'. I wonder who carried it to the top?

From the cairn a very worthwhile diversion leads 50yds west to the Millennium Cross (AD 2000) with interpretation panels. Just past the cross is a superb viewpoint.

From the cairn go east to the triangulation point, then turn left on the second path beyond. The path descends steeply, passing spoil heaps, to a gap in a wall and continues towards the isolated buildings of Eary

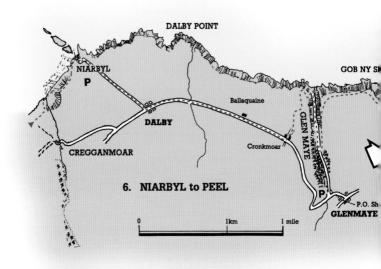

DALBY POINT

NIARBYL
P

GOB NY S

Ballaquaine

DALBY

CREGGANMOAR

Cronkmoar

GLEN MAYE

6. NIARBYL to PEEL

0   1km   1 mile

P

P.O. Sh
GLENMAYE

Cushlin, now an outdoor centre. A gap in an earth bank
is reached. The path heads left before reaching the house
to a signpost where a path from Eary Cushlin is crossed.
This crosspath is the old pony track which leads left to
Keeill-Lag-ny-Keeilley.

*The 'Keeill' was a little church built about
AD 430–700 on a small natural platform in the steep hillside. It had a foundation of stone, with walls of sods and
brushwood roofed with thatch. It was rectangular – 15ft
by 10ft – having a window to the east and a door to the
west. The hermit-priest lived in a small hut close by the
well and field, which he cultivated. The chapel was last
used for a funeral 100 years ago. The body was strapped
to the back of a pony and the mourners followed on foot.*

Enjoy the remoteness as you carry on down the left
side of the deep valley of Glen Mooar. A signpost at its

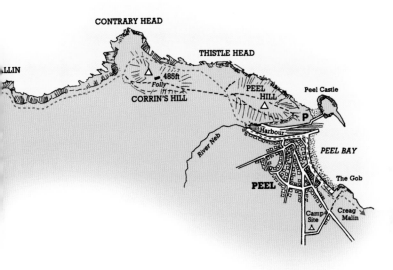

base indicates the way across. There is a good view into the bay and along the path to the *keeill* and the heather-clad slopes you have descended. The wry comment was made that the 'way of the gull' had turned into the 'way of the grouse'. As the descent continues the sound of the sea returns and a welcome signpost (w/m) confirms the route.

The path now turns right along the coast and descends into the small valley. Cross the fence and jump the stream. Descend a little, and the path rises round a shoulder and continues climbing through bracken with splendid views. A high ladder-stile (w/m) allows you to join a turf path, and as you wend your way upwards say a quiet thanks the owner who cares for the footpath so splendidly. Reach a rough lane but do not enter it. ▶

The lane leads to Cregganmooar and the road, but it is well worth keeping to the coastal footpath instead. At the Manx National Trust sign 'Creggan Moar Brooghs'

Note: The bad-weather alternative route joins here (animal water trough in the old lane).

The isolated Eary Cushlin below Cronk ny Arrey Laa

keep by the wall then bend left down to the headland. The view along the plunging coastline is spectacular, and barely less amazing are the four blending shades of pink scattered by the heather, thyme, sea-pink and stonecrop flowerheads. Pass through an old stone gateway and Niarbyl Bay comes into view. Keep on the cliffside of the fence to a gate with a public footpath sign. Turn down left on the signed path on concrete steps to a plank and stile. The onward path is overgrown, but soon a better path appears with a signpost. Go down left to a pretty waterfall at White Bay, and jump its stream as you turn right along the beach.

Crunch along the pebbles to the fence corner and turn right up the fenceside path to a final view of the sea-cliffs south to the Calf. Turn north above the void and along to Niarbyl Bay.

This bay with its tail of rocks and thatched cottage is most attractive. The tail is a ridge of rock protruding into the sea, where the Niarbyl and Lonan flags terminate with a flourish. The films Waking Ned *and* Five Children and It *were set here. The cottage above the bay was temporarily turned into a fine mansion for the filming.*

Turn up the steep winding lane to Dalby (telephone) and turn left on the main road for a mile. On reaching the hamlet of Cronkmooar look on the left for a tiny lane

White Bay and Niarbyl

Thatched cottage, Niarbyl, featured in the film 'Waking Ned'

between two cottages. Signpost (w/m). Turn left down the lane, through a five-barred gate into an enclosed pathway. Follow the right-of-way signs through the fields to the coast. The path now descends right into the rocky outlet of Glen Maye. Signpost (w/m).

The footbridge over the stream leads to a pretty rocky cove with a stone-arched cave.

Follow the wide path upstream along the verdant ravine of Glen Maye. The stream is now on your right. Look for a signpost on the left.

Half a mile up Glen Maye is a car park, toilets and the Waterfall Hotel.

A gate on your right gives access to the site of the Mona Erin Waterwheel, which was used to service a small lead mine in 1868. This is also the bottom entrance to Glen Maye, one of the island's national glens, which contains a beautiful waterfall and is well worth a visit.

At the signpost you will notice that our companion gull has caught two herrings. This marks the Bayr ny Skeddan, the Herring Way footpath from Peel to Castletown.

Turn left on the rising path, which crosses a stone stile and emerges from the trees to renew the seascape. Do not take the left fork. It leads down to the steps by the shelter in the bay. The path continues to rise and follows the cliff edge easily. Gradually gain height above a fine cliff, then as the path bends left do not be tempted into the field at a gap but keep ahead down the narrow path between the field and the cliff edge.

Stonechats and meadow pipits frequent the top of the cliff. If you listen for their chirping you will easily identify them, as they are not shy and continue their busy search of the gorse bushes scarcely heeding strangers.

The path now loses height, and away in the distance to the south there is a last glimpse of the Calf of Man. Ahead Corrin's Hill and its Folly seem close at hand.

Turn right into a field by means of a stile, and skirt round a boggy hollow. Regain the cliff edge again by means of another stile and carry on. A metal wicket gate is the next pause, soon followed by another and yet a third to reach the foot of Corrin's Hill. Signpost (w/m).

Turn left following the line of the wall. The path leaves the wall at a fin of rock to circle the hill on its seaward side. The path forks, but soon rejoins again, so go where fancy leads you. Continue along the cliff edge.

The path is straight and wide and rising. You walk this sublime terrace as a visitor. The gulls, which ride the air at eye level and preen on their soft balcony will allow you to share it briefly as you pass by. Go through a

Alternative Route

An alternative route taking you over Corrin's Hill is straightforward. From the signpost at the foot of the hill a prominent path leads directly to the tower and descends to the col on the other side. The tower was built in 1806 by Thomas Corrin, as a memorial to his family. It is 50ft high and the corners of the tower point to the four cardinal points of the compass. Corrin built the tower on the highest point of his land, 500ft above the sea. He, his wife and child are buried nearby.

Peel Castle from Peel Hill

wicket gate (w/m) and straight on to the col between Corrin's Hill and Peel Hill.

At the col two minor paths branch right towards Peel. The first is the official route, which descends steeply to the road and bridge. It is better to take your first view of Peel from the broad green track which rises over Peel Hill, so keep straight ahead as it swings away right, and as you come over the crest of the hill prepare for the grand finale. Peel Castle and the town enfold the picturesque harbour where the River Neb quietly enters the sea. Here is a spot to linger in the sunset, but if time is short turn right along the gravel track to the river bridge (w/m). Cross over the river into Peel.

Descending Peel Hill with the town spread out below

Peel to Kirk Michael

Distance:	7½ miles
Maximum height:	200ft

This section of the Raad ny Foillan is completely different to anything that has gone before, yet is equally scenic, interesting and enjoyable. On leaving Peel the colour of the cliffs changes to red sandstone. The profile of the inland hills is lower to the north, and the straight coast-line ahead hints at the long miles along the beach to where Jurby Point melts into a purple haze. The coast is followed for just over a mile. A short stretch on the road allows you to meet the old railway at the disused station of St Germaine's Halt. The old track carries the Raad ny Foillan through cuttings, over bridges and along parts of the coast visited only by birds and butterflies, as far as Glen Mooar. Here a descent is made down the beautiful glen with its lush woodland and cascading stream to the

Peel harbour

PEEL

TOURIST INFORMATION
Peel Town Commissioners, Derby Road. Tel: 01624 842341

ACCOMMODATION
B&B
Wide choice – see Tourist Information brochure for Peel
Campsite
Derby Road, Peel. Tel: 01624 842341, www.peelonline.net
Hot showers, laundry room, TV room, mid-April – 30 September (see map p88)

PUBLIC TRANSPORT
Bus
Runs from the Town Hall Peel – Douglas, Ramsey, Port Erin, Castletown, Airport, Glen Maye and Dalby for Niarbyl.

SERVICES
Full range of shops. Early closing Thursday.

COASTGUARD
Tel: 01624 844027

PLACES OF INTEREST
Peel Castle, open Easter–October
St German's Cathedral
House of Manannan, open all year
Kipper Factory

beach. High cliffs of conglomerate bound the sea, and after a mile along the beach the first break in these is Glen Wyllin, where the footpath climbs up onto the railway again and into Kirk Michael.

The Route
The town of Peel sits insignificantly alongside its proud castle and fascinating harbour, but in the shadow of huge chimneys taking fumes from the diesel-powered generating station. In the summer Viking longships ride at

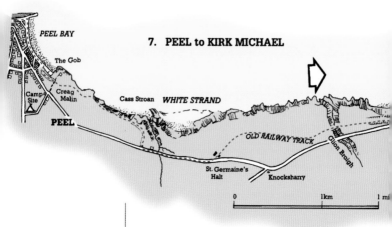

anchor, their fearsome prows nodding as they are disturbed by the wakes of their modern descendants.

From the river bridge waymark by a huge anchor, turn left and walk along the quayside. At the telephone box (w/m) turn right along the promenade. The Raad ny Foillan turns right up Walpole Road (w/m) then takes the path left. However, a short diversion along the promenade passes a cafe and toilets, accessed through a circular gateway. At the end of the promenade turn right immediately beyond the tennis courts, and a flight of steps leads to the waymarked path. When the wall ends a signpost ahead on the right indicates the continuing footpath beyond the bowling greens. The red sandstone cliffs have replaced the Manx slate and the coast now shows a different, though equally beautiful facet. Pass through the red gateway and past the foundations of an old building.

This was the Peveril Internment Camp, used during World War II. Those detained were under the 18B clause allowing 'any person suspected of enemy connections to be interned without trial'.

The paving ends at an iron wicket gate (w/m) and through this emerge onto the cliff path.

This is the Craig Malin headland where the Manx forefathers kept watch for the approach of the dreaded Cullock-Mac-Cullock, a notorious Galloway chief. According to an old Manx song he would 'carry off all not hot nor too heavy'.

Pass by a deep dyke then through a wicket gate. The path is easy, and your eyes will be continually drawn down the plunging cliffs to the sea. Do not become too distracted; bend right at Cass Struan.

Go through a wicket gate and descend the steps. Signpost (w/m). You can do a sneaky by-pass round the next wicket gate and carry on until you join the road. Turn left following the road north-east for just less than a mile until you arrive at the spot where an old railway track crosses the road at St Germaine's Halt. Signpost (w/m).

The railway, closed in 1968, ran a circuitous route from Douglas to Ramsey. It followed the valleys of the rivers Dhoo, Greeba and Neb westward as far as St Johns. Here a branch line continued along the Neb valley to Peel, and the Ramsey line pushed north-west to the coast. At Kirk Michael it turned inland again and

89

made its way east, passing through Ballough and Sulby, thence following the Sulby river to Ramsey. Your way follows the route of the old line for a while, the silent cuttings and embankments offering an undisturbed haven to a variety of wildlife. There are birds, butterflies and flowers in abundance.

I was enjoying the tranquillity of this old railway. My eyes were searching the track for flowers and I failed to notice the pride of the herd leading his cows to new pastures via the trackbed. I did not contest my right of way but almost literally flew down the embankment, over the ditch and fence to the safety of the field where I trespassed unashamed. My slightly less agile companion soon joined me muttering about the Way of the Gull being suddenly transformed into the Way of the Bull. Beware!

The green mound in the field on your left is an ancient earthwork, the site of a Pictish round house.

The old railway viaduct at Glen Mooar

Excursion to Spooyt Vane

Spooyt Vane is a pretty three-tiered waterfall. At the base of the old viaduct turn right up the glen. A cosseted path climbs gently to the site of Patrick's Chapel (8th–10th century), then continues to climb to the head of the waterfall. A series of steps on the left leads down the steep valley side allowing you to view the full length of the waterfall. Return to the base of the viaduct.

Being out of sight and sound of the sea you are more aware of the hills. From the south-east Slieau Ruy (1570ft), Coldon (1599ft), Sartfell (1490ft), Slieau Freoghane (1601ft) and Slieau Curn (1153ft), just north of Kirk Michael, form an impressive backcloth – but suddenly you gaze ahead onto wide beaches and are reminded you that you are still on the Raad ny Foillan.

A square tower at Kirk Michael is now in view. At the next lane the railway bridge has gone. Go down the steps on the left (w/m), cross the lane, then regain the railway. A succession of two gates, a lane, a little footbridge and another gate follow. Now prepare for a surprise. The old viaduct over Glen Mooar has gone and its guardian rail brings you to a sudden halt. The void is dramatic. A lone pier stands proud accusing the march of progress. ▶ Say *au revoir* to the railway and turn left down a steep path into Glen Mooar. Signpost (w/m).

At this point you can make the excursion to Spooyt Vane (see above).

In the shady glen turn left downstream to meet the road. Cross the road (w/m) and continue down by the hurrying stream. Cross over the footbridge by a ford and in a few minutes you will reach the beach. A toilet is in the car park.

The stream once powered a flax mill, and Weaver's Cottage (above on the left) was where linen and blankets were woven. The meadow bordering the sea with its flora is an area of special environmental interest.

At the beach turn right (w/m) and walk along the beach for a mile to Glen Wyllin. The sand is firm and passable at high tide, but a word of caution – from Douglas the sea has been your friendly neighbour, its tides and moods at a safe distance. At Glen Mooar you

The way takes to the beach at Glen Mooar

step into its territory. Be aware of the state of the tide and remember that a driving wind and a high tide may change circumstances. The cliffs are composed of glacial drift and are very unstable, so do not rely on them as an escape route. Local people use the beach daily and one gentleman said that he had only been stopped by the tide once. To quote the local workmen from the Department of Forests, Mines and Lands Board, 'except when a really high spring tide is backed by a storm wind you can always walk along the beach' (see section on tides, page 16).

Just walk and enjoy the blend of sounds and smells, shades and textures. This short stretch of beach is a small sample of things to come. The next gap in the cliffs is Glen Wyllin. Turn right up the glen (w/m) towards Kirk Michael.

Glen Wyllin campsite is a large site with full facilities in beautiful surroundings.

At the campsite the remains of the railway viaduct stand in the valley. Cross the bridge (w/m) and climb the steps under the topless viaduct to gain the old railway again. Follow the railway northward until you come to the vestige of the old level crossing on the outskirts of Kirk Michael.

Kirk Michael to Point of Ayre

Distance:	15 miles
Maximum height:	sea level

A short stretch on the old railway gives easy walking through pleasant rural landscape, then back to the beach and straight on past impressive sea cliffs. The coastline is not as straight as it appears on the map. The sand is firm, yet when the cliffs recede the heathland path is a welcome change. Check the state of the tide and wind speed. If the tide is approaching high watermark on a spring tide with a westerly gale-force wind, postpone your passage until the tide is on the ebb. The Jurby section of beach has a remote, exposed atmosphere. Jurby church offers unique historical interest. The change from glacial drift to sands and gravels gives a geologically

KIRK MICHAEL

TOURIST INFORMATION
Michael Village Commissioners, Tel: 01624 878836

PUBLIC TRANSPORT
Bus
Peel, Ramsey

SERVICES
Post Office, general store, butcher, (garage at N end of village sells paraffin), doctor, bank, cafe

PLACES OF INTEREST
Jurby Church; Spooyt Vane waterfall; Glen Mooar; Bishop's Court.
Ayres Nature Reserve Visitor Centre. Staffed by volunteers – open afternoons, seasonal.

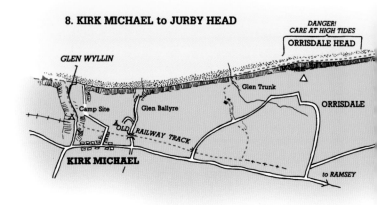

8. KIRK MICHAEL to JURBY HEAD

DANGER!
CARE AT HIGH TIDES

ORRISDALE HEAD

GLEN WYLLIN

Glen Trunk

ORRISDALE

Camp Site   Glen Ballyre

OLD RAILWAY TRACK

KIRK MICHAEL

to RAMSEY

young, gently undulating environment on which the Ayres Nature Reserve is situated. The Point of Ayre Lighthouse forms a worthy finish to this most northerly part of the Isle of Man. If you enjoy the company of seabirds, seals and plants you will find this section of the Raad ny Foillan outstanding.

The Route
Leave Kirk Michael by the long-gone level crossing and go through the fire station yard, still on the track of the old railway. The tower of Kirk Michael church is prominent on the right, with Slieau Curn (1184ft), Slieau Dhoo (1417ft) and Slieau Freoghane (1601ft) forming the horizon to the east. Keep on the railway over two footbridges, under two stone bridges and through a cutting, then look out for a gate on the left where a path crosses the line (w/m). Here the Raad ny Foillan says goodbye to the railway track. Turn left along an embanked footpath and through a wicket gate into a field. Follow the edge of the field to a gate and lane, signpost (w/m). Cross the lane to a bridle track, signpost (w/m).

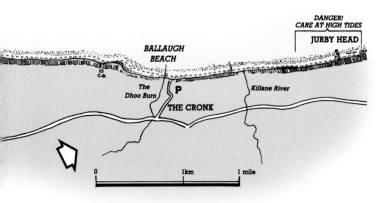

From the bridle track is a view north over the valley of Glen Trunk. A narrow road, known as the 'old trunk road' leads from the beach to an old limekiln. Limestone was brought by boat from the quarries at Scarlett Point and carried up to the kiln, where it was made into lime for agricultural use. The limestone was packed into the kiln with wood or charcoal, in alternate layers. It was then fired with a controlled air supply. This gave quicklime, which was slaked with water then used for agriculture.

Wind round the back of Ballarhenny Beg and go down, alongside a wall. Look how the wall is made in the traditional way, from earth set with pebbles and topped with turf. Descend into the deep cut, little valley of Glen Trunk. Cross the stream, and climb up to the signpost (w/m) then down left to the beach. Turn right, check the time and tide, then set the automatic pilot north-north-east for the Point of Ayre. Although the map indicates a 13½ mile trudge along the sand the reality is far better than the anticipation. The cliffs of Orrisdale Head soon pass by. They have been sculptured by water from glacial drift, with sand avalanches resembling giant

95

egg-timers counting the tides. An old coastguard beacon in the distance grows nearer as the cliffs lower. Along this stretch of beach I had the companionship of a friendly seal. Swimming a few yards from the breakers it followed my progress as far as the Ballaugh beach car park.

In 1697 at Ballaugh 'there was a remarkable wreck in this parish of a small vessel loaded with brandy, the first ever known on this island'. The taste for the spirit must have been rapidly acquired, for in 1698 Bishop Wilson arrived to find 'a rising tide of imported spirits'. He tried his best to turn back the tide but, like King Canute, had no success. The merchants of the island had set up a very lucrative business, importing good liquor at a ridiculously low rate of Manx duty. It was all legal and above board. They then transferred it to smugglers who passed it on at a profit. Ballaugh was one of the favourite beaches for the smugglers.

A gap allows the Dhoo Burn to enter the sea (w/m). On the north side of the car park is a sheltered picnic spot. The hamlet of Cronk is nearby. Continue along the beach to the gap in the cliffs where the Killane river enters the sea.

This is the nearest point south from which Jurby church can be visited, Sartfield being the next access path from the beach, 3 miles to the north. Jurby church is a prominent landmark.

In the porch of Jurby church is housed a fine collection of Manx crosses of 6th- to 12th-century origin. Casts of these are now exhibited in the Manx Museum. Two of the master sculptors working from AD 990–1050 were Gaut Bjornson, who was born on the Isle of Coll, Scotland, and Thorbjorn. It was Thorbjorn who carved the Sigurd crosses. The Sigurd slab tells of the slaying of Fafnir the dragon and other stories that are now immortalised in legend, stone and the well-known operas of Wagner. Plaques on the wall explain the crosses to the visitor and help to identify the figures. These crosses are unique, but the collection at Maughold is much more accessible for the Raad ny Foillan walker (see p.113).

After Jurby Head the cliffs rise in weird-shaped clay caverns and canyons. Passage along the beach should be possible throughout the year but there are always exceptions. Organise your passage of this section on an ebbing tide if you are in any doubt of the wave size and wind strength. The sheer cliffs are unstable, and attempts to escape that way are dangerous.

The Jurby wartime airstrip is now an industrial estate with 'Jurby Junk' and a small flying club. When the original concrete was being laid a burial mound was discovered. This was hurriedly opened. It was found to have items of great interest, so it was carefully recovered. After the war it was excavated and found to be the grave of a Scandinavian settler of great importance buried with his sword, shield and ornaments.

As the sand stretches on and on a few jolly songs and jaunty tales would not go amiss. The area through which you are now passing is rich in history and legend.

Let us contemplate an old Manx saw:
'When a man wants a wife, he wants but a wife,
But when he has a wife he wants a great deal'.

Between the surf and the cliffs at Jurby

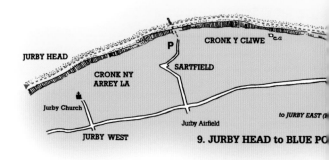

JURBY HEAD

CRONK NY ARREY LA

Jurby Church

JURBY WEST

P

SARTFIELD

CRONK Y CLIWE

Jurby Airfield

to JURBY EAST

9. JURBY HEAD to BLUE PO

A pipeline entering the sea indicates that you are level with Sartfield. A few yards inland is a sewage station with the current Bathing Water Quality Results posted outside. The cliffs lower, and marram grass consolidates the land from the sea. As the coastline veers an old coastguard station comes into view. Look for a signpost and (w/m) where a public footpath leads to the road. Another (w/m) at the Lhen heralds a change of activity. Here begins the Cronk y Bing Nature Reserve and it is possible to leave the sand and walk on a grassy shelf. Jump the stream at the outlet of the Lhen Trench, a man-made drainage channel. Just round the headland, with its old coastguard hut and accompanying wartime pill-box, is a waymark and a gap in the dunes, which leads to the raised beach and the Blue Point car park. Alongside the car park is a clay pigeon shooting range. Do not enter if the red flag is flying.

Continue on the path between the wall-fence and the edge of the dunes. Here it is easier walking along the turf. This is a welcome change, as the beach has become soft and pebbly. Duck under an old fence and carry on ahead. The lighthouse you have awaited with anticipation since Spanish Head now comes into view. The sight

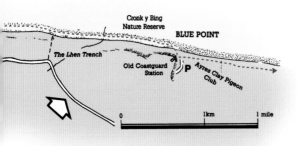

of the Point of Ayre puts the spring back into your feet. Take your choice between the beach or the easier walking on the heath.

Marram grass was pulled by hand in large quantities and used as thatching in the north of the island. Today its chief use is to bind the mobile sand with its matted roots and allow the clumps of sea holly to grow.

At Rue Point a wooden walkway gives access to the car park information panel (w/m). It can be easily missed if walking out on the beach. You have now entered the Ayres Nature Reserve and recreation area. There is no camping, and Motorhomes are allowed only at this end.

Wrecks have made some strange contributions to Man, but the strangest must have come with the schooner Hooton *in 1805. She sailed from Whitehaven on the Cumbrian coast and was wrecked on Rue Point. Amongst the passengers' luggage was a box containing several hedgehogs, a species previously unknown to the island. The rescued animals were distributed as pets amongst the local residents and have bred so prolifically that they are now common throughout the island.*

From Rue Point it is pleasant to walk on the heathland, stabilized and supporting a wealth of wildlife, just

10. BLUE POINT to POINT OF AYRE

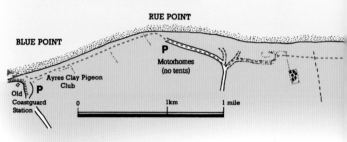

behind the sand dunes. For a while a narrow concrete road makes easy going; when it swings away inland, keep ahead. On the left are dunes and the beach. Little terns, a protected species, are ground-nesting birds and all visitors are asked to tread carefully. If you want to examine the flora of this special environment this is the place to do so.

The Manx Nature Conservation Trust has set up a Nature Trail and Visitors' Centre. The area is one favoured by rare plants and birds in need of conservation. It is composed of different environments, varying with the measure of consolidation achieved by the sands and gravels. There are examples of shingle, dune, heath and raised beach. In winter the water table is very high, and for short periods parts stand flooded by fresh water. Information boards tell you of the wildlife to be seen in the area.

When opposite a stand of pine trees in the middle distance to your right, the Ayres plantation, a good path runs in a trough parallel to the beach and makes faster and more interesting going. The next landmark is a sign-post – public footpath to Allaggarrett. The roof of the

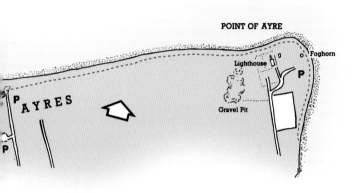

Ayres Visitors' Centre is in sight. It is open every afternoon in the season (no toilets).

Leave the Ayres Visitors' Centre by the paved footpath 50yds inland from a point opposite the building and continue along a well-trodden path to the lighthouse.

Curlews, oystercatchers, ringed plovers, little terns and common terns nest in these marram dunes, and once again a notice begs walkers to watch their step and not to linger, so as not to disturb the nesting birds. Remember that the longer you take to pass, the longer the eggs or young are unprotected and exposed to the cold or predators. The black-headed gulls like to nest in a disused gravel pit next to the refuse dump.

The Point of Ayre Lighthouse is now automatic. The Isle of Man Lights are controlled not by Trinity House, but by the Northern Lights Board of Scotland. The Point of Ayre Lighthouse was built between 1815 and 1818 by Robert Louis Stevenson's grandfather.

There is a Post Office, a restaurant and a toilet block at Bride village (3 miles).

Point of Ayre to Ramsey

Distance:	7 miles
Maximum height:	sea level

At the Point of Ayre the traces of old salt and gravel workings and a more recent landfill site are rather unpleasant. (The bus turns at the landfill site gateway.)

This is a popular place for sea fishermen where, apart from a short period of slack tide, the water pours round the point in a 3½ knot race. Seabirds dive into the agitated water and ride on the currents. The proximity of the revolting tip becomes insignificant.

Point of Ayre lighthouse

The buoy out to sea is the Whitestone Buoy, which marks the position of the Bahama Bank. This sandbank stretches east for 6 miles offshore.

The fine quality of the Raad ny Foillan is quickly rekindled. As you travel south the cliffs rise and, as the glacial drift boulder clay is met, become more spectacular. Check the tide and wind speed.

The scene ahead gains interest as the hills, North Barrule, Slieau Managh and Snaefell, grow nearer. Ramsey Bay sweeps east to terminate in Maughold Head. This sets you looking forward in anticipation of enjoying its footpath. The walking, all on or near the beach, becomes firmer and easier. Ramsey is reached perhaps more quickly than anticipated.

RAMSEY

TOURIST INFORMATION
Ramsey Town Commissioners, Town Hall, Bowring Road, Ramsey. Tel: 01624 810146

ACCOMMODATION
B/B Ramsey – wide choice – see Tourist Information brochure.

PUBLIC TRANSPORT
Bus
Starts from the Depot, Queen's Pier Road
Electric train
April to October. Station Albert Street.

SERVICES
Full range of shops, supermarket. Early closing – Wednesday
Coastguard, Tel: 661664
Heated swimming pool, with cafe and public showers. Hospital.

PLACES OF INTEREST
Rural Life Museum; Wild Life Park Ballaugh; Mooragh Park; Celtic Music and Dance Festival

The Route

Being at sea level the viewpoint is not the best, yet on a clear day the Galloway hills seem very close (Burrow Head, Galloway, 18 miles).

In the 19th century borings were made at the Point of Ayre in the search for coal. They were unsuccessful as far as the coal was concerned, but salt was found at a depth of 600ft in the Triassic marls below the glacial drift. Water was pumped down, and brine brought to the surface was piped to the salt works at Ramsey. This worked well for a while, but by 1956 salt obtained in this way proved uneconomical and the workings were abandoned.

Pass the foghorn and turn south (w/m). In spite of notices sightseers drive onto the unstable beach and it is not unusual to see a car stuck hub-deep in the large pebbles. A decade or so ago gravel was being taken for

103

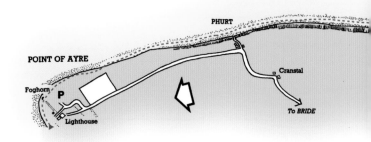

road building, but this gave rise to erosion further south along the coast and had to be stopped. Away to the south the distant peak of North Barrule above Ramsey beckons. Follow a path along the edge of the heath, looking out for the elusive remains of the concrete pier.

Opposite the landfill site metal rods and pieces of concrete, seen only at very low tide, appear on the beach. These are the remains of a concrete ship. The Burscough was built in Preston, Lancashire, and was launched in 1921. She was a motor vessel of 229 tons,

Looking back north to Shellag Point

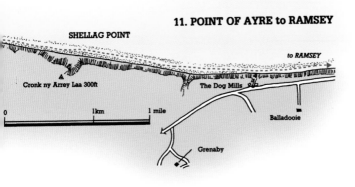

11. POINT OF AYRE to RAMSEY

SHELLAG POINT

to RAMSEY

Cronk ny Arrey Laa 300ft

The Dog Mills

Balladooie

Grenaby

0   1km   1 mile

and as steel was in short supply she was built of rein-
forced concrete. Her short life was dogged with trouble.
She made a successful voyage to Kingstown with a cargo
of coal, then the difficulties started. Her engines failed
her and she had to be towed back to Preston from
Douglas. In 1924 her fittings were removed and the hulk
towed to the Point of Ayre. It was sunk to form part of the
jetty, which has since been demolished.

The shingle is difficult to walk on, so stay on the turf
as long as possible. Pass by a tin hut and launching ramp
where the hook of an old anchor lies half-buried in
the sand.

After passing the cottages of Phert ('port') low cliffs
begin to develop as the blown sands and gravels give
way to the red conglomerates once more. The beach
gravel gradually gives way to strips of sand and pebbles,
making the walking firmer. Looking onward, Maughold
Head beyond Ramsey forms the southern side of Ramsey
Bay on the horizon.

Before going further, check the state of the tide.
There is little room for walking between the waves and
the cliff at high tide. Take care when approaching the

Ramsey harbour

foot of the cliffs, as the cliffs are muddy, waterlogged and highly unstable, sending down fine granite boulders of Scottish origin from time to time.

From the beach Shellag Point stands out as a definite feature, although the coast appears straight on the map. The first major break in the cliffs as you progress beyond Shellag Point shows that you have reached Kionlough. Steps and a waymark with a signpost 'Dog Mills' point to the main road access. Carry on along the sand until you come to the end of the Ramsey promenade (toilets and café in the park right).

There are two local explanations of this strange name. The first tells of a dog in a trundle wheel, used to raise water in times of drought. The second speaks of the old flour mill, its stones making the noise of a whining dog.

If you have a streak of Tuareg in you, you can carry on along the sand as far as the harbour. But if you have spent enough time in low gear, empty your boots, change up and stride out firmly along the promenade into Ramsey. At the harbour continue to follow the road round to the right. There is a water tap on a grey brick wall to the left just round the bend. Turn left over the swing bridge (opened 1892) between the inner and outer harbours (w/m).

Ramsey to Laxey

Distance:	13 miles
Maximum height:	650ft

Throughout this section an interesting mixture of cliff and glen, meadow and lane is met. The sudden change from glacial drift to the Manx slates is clearly seen in the sheer rugged cliffs of the coast, the change of vegetation and gradient of the Raad ny Foillan.

The sections of road walking are mainly on quiet lanes with interesting hedgerows or wide views. The highlights of the section must be the traverse of Maughold Head and the descent of lovely Glen Cornaa. An excursion into Dhoon Glen, one of the most beautiful on the island, would warrant extra time spent in the area.

The walking is rocky in places and demands care. The footpath makes and descends 1200ft in three visits to sea level from the coastal plateau. The gradients are so easy that they mostly pass unnoticed.

The footpath passes by Maughold church and the Ballafoyle Cairn, sites of prime historical interest.

The Route

At the harbour bridge (w/m) turn left towards the sea and follow the side of the harbour, bending left at the market place along the East Quay.

I cannot resist the fascination of a working harbour, with boats of all shapes and sizes and the nautical flavour reflected in the buildings – the Isle of Man Steam Packet Company and the Harbourmaster's office, complete with barometer and tide timetable (useful if you are doing the Raad ny Foillan anticlockwise).

Turn right along the South Promenade passing the swimming pool cafe and toilets to the Queen's Pier

12. RAMSEY to PORT MOOAR

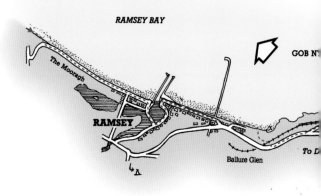

RAMSEY BAY

The Mooragh

GOB N'

RAMSEY

Ballure Glen

To D

(w/m). **At most states of tide** go down the steps and along the beach until twin arches and a stream are seen. Go through the first arch, pass the footpath and continue up the Ballure Glen by the path alongside its stream. Cross over the footbridge. A zigzag path climbs up through pleasant gardens to a railway crossing.

The Manx electric railway runs from Ramsey to Douglas. From May to September there are five trains daily in each direction. Although the rolling stock with its leather seats and tassels may look quaint, there is nothing sedate about the speed with which it hurtles round the corners and darts in and out of the cuttings sounding its hooter. You will cross its track many times before you reach Douglas, so take care. Before you cross the line look and listen.

Cross the railway line to the main road (w/m). ◀

Keep along the main road for about ¾ mile then fork left towards Maughold (w/m). Cross a railway bridge and

At unusual high tide from the Queen's Pier keep on the road until in 100yds it joins the main road to Laxey. Continue left towards Laxey until you cross over the railway bridge and find the way-mark at the path junction.

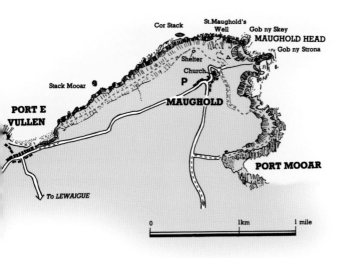

look for a waymark and signpost, Port e Vullen, on your left.

The onward route is impassable at high tide. Turn left (Manx National Trust: Gob ny Rona) and take the green path ahead to a small car park. If the tide is in, stay on the road to * (see below).

This must be a spot loved by local photographers, for you can see the coastline stretching away north to the Point of Ayre, the lighthouse a tiny white pin, cushioned on the horizon.

Follow the sea wall round the headland. A fine view of Maughold Head can be enjoyed until steps lead down to tidal section and the beach at Port e Vullen. Signpost.

The outcropping rocks on the beach have been eroded into strange and flowing shapes, the exposed strata in its pristine colours.

A concrete ramp from the beach will lead you to the road. A cameo of Queen Victoria is mounted on the

Walkers try to reach Porth-y-Vullen but the tide is too high

gable of a house to the right. At the road is a signpost (w/m). Turn left up the road for 300yds.* Leave the road at a wicket gate (w/m) (signpost: Maughold Brooghs), and another wicket gate takes you back into the wild.

A herd of Loaghtan, the four-horned Manx sheep, belonging to Manx Heritage live here, so you may get a chance to admire them. The male is a small but handsome fellow with four re-curved horns and a coffee-coloured fleece. The female has two shorter horns. They are goat-like in their agility and well suit their rugged surroundings. I saw another fine herd of Loaghtan in Shropshire, but their luxurious field did not complement them like the rugged coast of their isle.

At the start of the path a sign warns you of rough walking to come. Do not be alarmed; the path, with Stack Mooar below, is broad and easy compared with the paths you have already encountered. As the path begins to climb, look back where Albert Tower appears in silhouette.

The tower commemorates the spot from which the Prince Consort viewed Ramsey in 1847. The royal party were to have landed at Douglas but, as often happens when royalty approach the Isle of Man, the ancient necromancer and Sea King Manannan McLir threw a curtain of mist around Douglas and Queen Victoria and Prince Albert were diverted to Ramsey. By the time the reception committee had reached Ramsey the Prince had climbed the hill, admired the view, and gone.

Queen Elizabeth II and Prince Philip visited the island on a beautiful sunny day in 1955. As the royal yacht approached the island a thick fog settled. As the Queen sailed away in the evening the fog evaporated to leave clear skies. Her Majesty made a visit on Tynwald Day 2003 in fine weather. Draw your own conclusions.

Look ahead where Cor Stack, down at sea level, helps you appreciate the invisible 300ft contour you are crossing, and as you continue to gain height North Barrule comes into view, but do not stop here because shelter and a viewpoint indicator soon come along, complete with seat.

The footpath descends to a wall corner. Keep by the wall. Continue to lose height to a Manx National Trust sign. Go through the gap in a cross-wall into a grassy hollow. A wicket gate ahead gives access to a redundant car park (w/m) signpost.

A path branching left down the cliff leads to St Maughold's Well and Maughold Head. On the cliffs below is a large kittiwake colony. It is a popular spot with four types of auks breeding here.

Go down the lane leading from the car park. Turn right along the minor road, then left at the graveyard. To reach the toilets in Maughold village, go through the churchyard to the village green. The toilets are up a narrow lane on the right.

Maughold may be a tiny community but it has a huge hoard of history within sight of its village green.

North Barrule from Maughold Brooghs

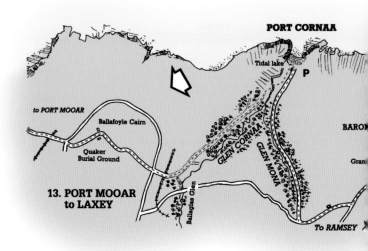

Maughold Head is the furthest point east on the Isle of
Man. Its light- house is not visible at the moment from
the Raad ny Foillan, but it will come into view presently.
Cliffs of Barrule slates and quartz-veined grits fall sheer to
the sea, where they are washed by tidal currents which
tend to push north-east up the Irish Sea. These currents
brought Maughold its name and the island one of its
most revered ancestors.

Tradition tells of Machud or MacCuill, a pagan
robber, whom St Patrick converted to Christianity. As a
penance for his former sins St Patrick ordered that
Machud should be chained, set adrift in a wicker coracle
and left to the mercy of God. The coracle drifted out to
sea and was carried by the tide to the headland where it
was dashed to pieces on its jagged rocks. Two men
chanced to be at hand. They pulled Machud from the
breakers, and as he touched land his chains fell off and
he was freed. They climbed the cliffs, and when Machud

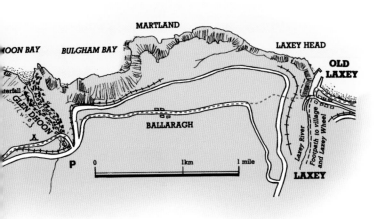

reached the grassy slopes he fell on his knees and gave thanks for his deliverance. On that spot a spring gushed from the ground. It was named St Maughold's Well. Machud spent the rest of his life in the service of God. Helped by the local people he built a little church on the headland and travelled around preaching and teaching. He became bishop to the island and was known as St Machud or St Maughold. He died in AD 553, so it is said, and was buried in his churchyard.

Along the side-wall of the churchyard at Maughold a shelter has been made for the collection of ancient stones. Forty-four pieces, crosses and slabs dating from the 6th–12th centuries, are displayed. The Scandinavian crosses continue the story of Sigurd. One other cross, made of St Bees sandstone, is the Maughold Village Cross. It has been moved from the village green into the church. Its special interest is the carved shield with the

The old Market Cross at Maughold (now inside the church)

113

A family enjoys the path at Maughold Head

three legs of Man. This is one of the oldest representations of the well-known national emblem, the other being on the Manx sword of state. This sword was carried into battle by Olaf Godredson when he fought the Moors of Spain in 1230. The same sword is carried by the Governor in procession on Tynwald Day.

The church itself is of great interest. The porch has a Celtic arch springing from a capitol with a human face on the front and beasts at each side. There is more 10th-century work to be seen. The font is very large and must have been meant for total immersion. In the churchyard, which was once fortified by a wall and ditch, are the ruins of two ancient keeills. Unexpectedly, this esteemed spot is connected with pirate's treasure. A gold coin was found in the church wall. It was dated to Louis le Debonnaire, son of Charlemagne. It is presumed to be part of a Scandinavian pirate hoard and is now in the Manx Museum.

From the signpost (w/m) at the corner of Maughold churchyard turn left down the green lane, through a gate on a right bend and continue past a signpost on a left bend. The lane ends at a stone stile. Go straight on to a high ladder-stile. The extra few feet in height gained by the stile is useful. From the top of the stile the Maughold Head Lighthouse can be seen on the left. Turn left and zigzag down to the tiny cove of Dhyrnane. Your path circles the cove and climbs steps to traverse above the rocks. Just beyond the cove a flat-topped rock platform protrudes into the sea from path level.

This is the place from which to examine Maughold Head. A natural rock arch and two pinnacles known as the Twin Cletts give sport to rock climbers. Grey Atlantic seals can be seen around the rocks.

Walk on along the grass path into the larger bay of Port Mooar. Take to the beach to reach the car park.

Here the Raad ny Foillan has to leave the coast for a while. Make your way up the narrow road to a minor road signpost (w/m). Turn left and go along this road for ¾ mile crossing over the railway bridge at Ballajora. At the main road go almost straight across (w/m) and up the hill. On the crest is a grove of pines.

The Ballafoyle Cairn, the remains of a Neolithic burial site, can be seen on the left of the lane, together with the site of an ancient keeill. On the right is the Quaker's burial ground Rhullick-ny-Quakeryn. The Quakers were severely persecuted by Bishop Barrow (1663) and many died in dreadful circumstances.

The height from this lane presents a fine panorama of the central highlands. The wooded line of upper Glen Cornaa draws the eye to Snaefell, with North Barrule to its right and Slieau Duyr on its left.

Cross a wider road (w/m) and descend into the deep valley of Glen Cornaa. Here you meet the railway again, and do not forget that it is very much alive on this side of the island. Go straight down the lane, signpost (w/m), along the glenside. A bridle track veers right. Keep straight on at the gates, and on through a grove of beautiful beech trees. Ignore a track forking left and keep straight on. There are waterfalls and pools in the river, an ideal picnic spot that invites you to stay a while by the stream. Carry on through a gate.

On the right an old concrete ruin can be seen amongst the trees. It never grew beyond the foundations as its purpose was nipped in the bud. A Swedish gentleman began the building in the middle of the 19th century. He intended to manufacture Belite (gunpowder) and export it from a tiny quay, which he built in the bay. However, the Manx Government discovered his intentions and rapidly brought his activities to a halt, leaving nature to disguise the stark remains.

Cross over the bridge to gain access to the beach. It is a storm beach with huge terraces of wave-flung pebbles. The turf between the bridge and the beach floods at high tide, signpost (w/m). Leave Port Cornaa by the road up Glen Mona.

Walk up the glen road and carry straight on where a narrow road joins at a ford (1¼ miles). At the T-junction turn left (w/m), then cross the railway to the main road (w/m). Turn left and left again in 150yds. Ignore the lane, also on the left, to Dhoon Quarry.

The Dhoon granite has been quarried for many years. This grey, mottled granite was exported as granite setts for the roads of Lancashire and Yorkshire. It is used as road metal on Man today and can be seen in local buildings.

Go straight on over the next level crossing. A reassuring waymark is welcome along the next 3¼ mile stretch of road.

An idyllic pool in Glen Cornaa

The valley to seaward is Dhoon Glen, leading to Dhoon Bay, a renowned beauty spot and well worth a visit. There is a waterfall which falls 160ft in three leaps; some interesting old mine workings where the stone housing for a 50ft waterwheel remains; and a beach where the Dhoon flags form attractive rock pools. If you follow the path by the stream down to the beach a return to the Raad ny Foillan can be made by crossing the stream on the beach; a path soon turns right and climbs steeply to a viewpoint. This is a good place for bird-watching – fulmar and petrels nest on the cliffs. Ignore a small path on the right, and keep on the main path along the cliff top which soon swings sharp right inland over-looking the glen. At a stile onto the minor road you are back on the Raad ny Foillan. The circuit down Dhoon Glen is about 3 miles and takes 1 1/4 hours.

A ladder-stile over a wall is the next thing to look for. Signpost Ballaragh Road (w/m). Go over the stile and through the gate. Follow the fence wall to the far field corner. A stile in the fence corner leads into bracken. You are not lost; follow the wall to another stile and stone steps to cross the railway line. Cross the main road. Mount a stile into the field. Signpost. Keep up by the wall to another sign and turn left on the minor road.

Having gained some height, there is a splendid view over Dhoon Glen and the coast to the north-east, Slieau Lhean and Slieau Duyr to the north-west. From here you can study your progress south.

Keep along this minor road for 1 3/4 miles. Ignore a signpost to 'coast road' (w/m) and 'public footpath to main road' (w/m). The waymarks confirm that the road is still the way. As the hill steepens, look for a waymark on the left. The road bends away to the right. Leave the road and go down a hedged bridle track. Cross the main road (waymarks to right). The valley of the River Laxey is before you. Take the descending footpath and cross the railway. The footpath narrows and steepens then joins an alpine-style road. Take no notice of the signpost on the left and you will arrive in a minute at the Laxey harbour bridge.

Laxey to Douglas

Distance:	9½ miles
Maximum height:	350ft

The Raad ny Foillan now passes through the most densely populated part of the island. This section contains some stretches on the main road, which the authorities know are unsatisfactory and are doing their best to improve. Having said this, let me quote the words of a fellow walker 'I walked from Douglas to Laxey along the Raad ny Foillan and much enjoyed it – to my surprise'. The path visits the peaceful havens of Garwick Bay and Port Groudle. The lanes and paths go over Clay Head through the Ballanette Conservation Area with extensive views. The descent of the Onchan Head moor is a sudden surprise. Almost last, but not least, the generosity of the local residents in allowing the footpath to go through their gardens should be mentioned. The final stroll along the Douglas promenade is a satisfying completion of the circuit.

The Route

The estuary of the River Laxey forms the picturesque harbour. The bridge is the place to leave the Raad ny Foillan if you want to visit the famous Laxey Wheel, stay or shop in the village, visit the woollen mill or camp for the night.

Cross the river bridge and turn left (w/m) along the picturesque harbour side to the sea wall. (Toilets at the harbour.)

Laxey means 'salmon' in Manx. The number of salmon in the Dhoo, Glass, Santon and Sulby rivers has dwindled, and all river and sea fishing for salmon and brown trout is banned. The fish are now returning. The Board of Agriculture and Fisheries has a breeding station

LAXEY

TOURIST INFORMATION
Laxey Village Commissioners, New Road, Laxey. Tel: 01624 861241/862623
Laxey Heritage Trust. Tel: 01624 862007

ACCOMMODATION
B&B Wide choice – see Tourist Information brochure.

PUBLIC TRANSPORT
Bus
To Douglas and Ramsey
Electric train
To Douglas and Ramsey
Mountain railway
To Snaefell summit

SERVICES
Shops. Early closing Thursday
Laxey Promenade Cafe open March – September

PLACES OF INTEREST
The Laxey Wheel and Mines Trail; St George's Woollen Mills (sells woollen socks)

at Maughold from which it restocks the rivers. A fisherman I spoke to was more interested in his catch of scallops and queenies which he took to the Island Seafare at Port St Mary.

The harbour is built Cornish style. The inner harbour dries out at low tide and is sheltered by Laxey Head and a sturdy stone pier. There are public toilets on the pier. The short promenade has a shelter and cafe open March–September.

Turn right along the promenade as far as the toilets.

If the tide is high a signpost indicates a zigzag path behind the toilets, leading up the hillside to the road. Here you turn left and soon fork left again on the main road (Footpath sign). This diversion is the worst part of the Raad ny Foillan, so grit your teeth and follow the

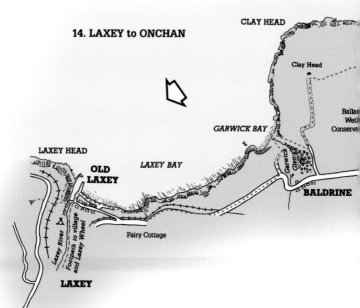

14. LAXEY to ONCHAN

CLAY HEAD

Clay Head

Ballan
Wetl
Conserva

GARWICK BAY

LAXEY HEAD

LAXEY BAY

OLD
LAXEY

Garwick
Glen

BALDRINE

Laxey River

Footpath to village
and Laxey Wheel

Fairy Cottage

LAXEY

busy main road. Cross the railway and meet
the low tide route at the w/m.

*The path leaves Laxey
beach at sloping rocks*

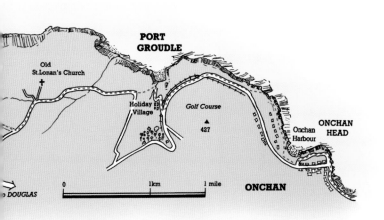

If the tide is low or on the ebb go along the beach. The path up the impregnable high cliffs is difficult to locate, but be assured – it is there. You are making for a promontory of large seaweed-covered rocks, Gob y Rheynn, about ¼ mile along the beach. A rough guide is a clump of pine trees growing on the cliff top at Fairy

The path to Fairy Cottage leaves Laxey beach up shelving rocks to a groove in the cliff

Celtic wheel cross at
Old Kirk Lonan

Cottage. Do **not** go up an obvious break with steps approached along a sandy break in the base rocks. Part of this path has badly eroded away and a warning notice appears at the top. Pass this and locate a cleft sloping up from clean, shelving rock and just to the right of the promontory face. At the base of the cleft 'Fairy' is painted on the rock wall. Approach the cliff easily over the smooth base rock to a sound, unexposed path, with steps and handrails, which leads up the cliff to a road. Turn right on a surfaced lane, cross the railway and join the main road. Turn left (w/m).

Walk along the road and just before the road bends right, look for a lane on the left, signpost (w/m). Go down this lane to Garwick Bay, a tiny, peaceful haven from the traffic and more like the Way of the Gull. Cross the stone slab bridge by the boathouse (w/m). Climb the side of the wooded valley to Baldrine.

At the single-track road turn left, still uphill (w/m and a sign to Clay Head). Keep on this road to Clay Head Farm – Private Drive. Go through this gate and in 25yds turn right (w/m) into a pathway. There is a view north to Maughold Head. At a gate the path widens to a green track. Clay Head is now part of the Ballannette Conservation, Wetlands Area.

The farmland you are walking through is farmed using environmental and ecological methods, which include a complete ban on chemicals. No fields are cut for hay until August to leave field-nesting birds, such as the lapwing, undisturbed. Several rare plants have appeared and are flourishing.

The next waymark is on Clay Head with an extensive mountain panorama. Follow the track to its end and turn right in front of the buildings. Go along the access road to a paved area and seat. This is an ideal spot to linger and enjoy the lakes and birds – choughs, tufted duck and snipe – and, of course, the seabirds, all framed in a backdrop of mountains.

The Ballannette Conservation, Wetlands Area have been developed by a trust set up in memory of Annette Clague who died tragically in 1995 at the age of 21 years (further information at www.scs.co.im/ballannette).

Continue along the access lane to join a minor road, signpost (w/m). Turn left and keep on the minor road, which leads pleasantly between hedgerows for 1¼ miles.

A quarter of a mile along this road a lane branches off on the left, then right to Old Kirk Lonan. It is but a short distance and should not be missed by anyone with a liking for history.

Old Kirk Lonan or 'the church by the shore' is dedicated to St Onan, or Adamnan, an Irish saint who was the Abbot of Iona in 679. The walls to be seen today date back to the 12th century, but the site is much older, dating back to the fifth century. In the churchyard stands a Celtic cross of the 7th–9th century in its original position. Its decorative bands of plait-work can be clearly seen. Near the church is the old baptismal well, used before the days of the font.

The height gained brings views of the hills to the west as they recede into the distance.

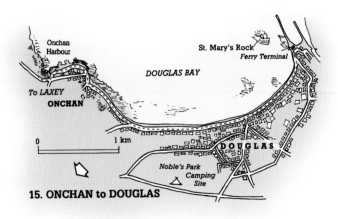

15. ONCHAN to DOUGLAS

At a right bend keep straight on, using a footpath that soon crosses the narrow-gauge Groudle Glen railway, built 1896, and now restored and run by local enthusiasts. Descend to cross the stream by Groudle beach. Leave Port Groudle by the road, which winds up steeply through the holiday village, and turn left when you reach the main road.

The mile along this road is not unpleasant. The traffic has taken the inland road through Onchan and the Raad ny Foillan has only to share it with a few cars and the electric railway. The enjoyment is by no means over. The views keep improving with every step as you round the hill and gain height. To the north Port Groudle and Clay Head appear, whilst Douglas to the south heralds journey's end. It was only when I had Douglas spread before me from this vantage point that I realised it took its name from the junction of the River Dhoo with the River Glass.

Robert the Bruce visited the Isle of Man in 1313. He landed at Ramsey with his army and set off for Castletown to attack the Scandinavian stronghold, on the site where Castle Rushen now stands. As you are familiar with the distance, you will appreciate that by the time

Port Groudle

Bruce and his army had reached Douglas they were very tired and in no fit state to carry on to Castletown, let alone fight a battle. But Douglas was even then renowned for its hospitality. Bruce and his army spent the night in the nunnery. They went on to Castletown next day to win the battle and annexe the island to Scottish rule.

At Onchan the path keeps on the cliff edge below the houses

A waymark and signpost by the 'Onchan' sign show where to turn left off the road. Go down a narrow footpath with wooden steps, which appears to be taking you down the moor and straight off the sheer cliff and into the sea. The path soon levels out and you feel that you are back on the real Raad ny Foillan again. The path runs on the cliff edge as you progress.

Go round a deep zawn, the footpath still keeping to the cliff edge, to join the road again above the deep inlet of Onchan Harbour. Turn left and left again into Sea Cliff Road which traverses Onchan Head. At the main road keep left along the pavement (w/m) and on to the Douglas promenade. At the southern end of the promenade is the harbour from which you started.

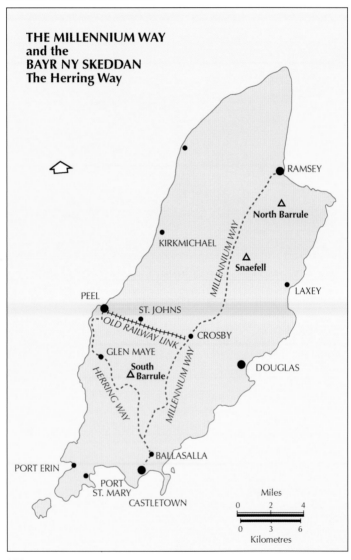

THE MILLENNIUM WAY
and the
BAYR NY SKEDDAN
The Herring Way

RAMSEY

△ **North Barrule**

KIRKMICHAEL

△ **Snaefell**

PEEL

LAXEY

ST. JOHNS

OLD RAILWAY LINK

CROSBY

GLEN MAYE

South
△ **Barrule**

MILLENNIUM WAY

HERRING WAY

DOUGLAS

BALLASALLA

PORT ERIN

PORT
ST. MARY

CASTLETOWN

Miles
0   2   4

0   3   6
Kilometres

THE MILLENNIUM WAY
(Ramsey to Castletown)

Twenty-three miles (approximately)

The Millennium Way was the first long-distance footpath to be established in the Isle of Man. It was timed to coincide with the millennium year of Tynwald in 1979. It follows as closely as possible the ancient route of the kings from Ramsey to Castletown. Ramsey, being on the Sulby River, formed a safe anchorage favoured by the Norse kings. Castle Rushen, Castletown, was the royal residence. The route also passed the ancient site of Tynwald at Keeill Abban.

After a steep climb out of the Sulby valley, open moorland gives fine views out over the northern plain and across the sea to Galloway and the English Lake District. The Way then winds across the western flanks of Snaefell, the cunning line leaving you almost unaware of the mountain road above, and undisturbed by the collection of hardware on Snaefell's summit. The infant River Sulby is crossed and a rough ascent to the watershed between Beinn-y-Phott and Carraghan made, yet the ancient pathway reappears from time to time. An easy descent to the Baldwin valley exchanges the mountain vistas for gentle scented lanes and picturesque rural miniatures.

At Crosby the Way is forced onto the road for 3½ miles. At St Mark's a traverse of farmland leads west until another short stretch of road drops the Way into the beautiful Silverburn valley. This excellent finish to the walk is shared by the Bayr ny Skeddan (the Herring Way). Footpaths by the river lead through Silverburn Glen to Ballasalla and through the fields by the river to Castletown.

The route is well waymarked throughout its length although the original waymarks, a concrete post with the badge, have almost disappeared. The sheep seem to use them as rubbing posts.

It is possible to combine the best parts of the Millennium Way with the Herring Way by using the Heritage Trail, a footpath along the old railway from Crosby to Peel. This gives a really fine walk through the centre of the island, and is well worth a special visit.

Ramsey to Crosby

Distance:	12¾ miles
Maximum height:	1500ft

The Millennium Way starts just over a mile from Ramsey along the road to Peel. Leave Ramsey by Lezayre Road, and if you walk on the right you will soon pass an old milestone informing you that Castletown is 25 miles away.

The land to the north is flat, while to the south the slopes of Sky Hill rise almost from the tarmac. The road is following the junction of the sands and gravels with the Barrule slates of the hills.

Look on the left for the first waymark. It shares a signpost with a fingerpost pointing to the Mountain Road. A bridle track winds up the wooded hillside of Sky Hill (*skogarfjall* meaning 'wooded hill'). In the springtime bluebells, stitchwort, violets and wood sorrel line the

The Watershed Cairn

way. On leaving the trees behind, the path becomes a sheltered, sunken way. The banks are crowned with gorse – high enough to lift the wind, low enough to permit an outlook – and as you gain height the panoramas are vast. Pass a little spring on the left, come to the Sky Hill boundary gate and spend a few minutes enjoying the view.

To the north-west Jurby church stands white on the coastline. North on a clear day across the sea lies Galloway, with Burrow Head and Cairnsmore of Fleet, and The Merrick nestling behind and between them on the edge of the horizon. The Point of Ayre Lighthouse can just be seen peeping over the Bride hills, and away to the east the mountains of Lakeland are visible, their profiles unfamiliar to those who usually approach them from the M6.

The slopes of Sky Hill that you have just climbed are steeped in Manx history. If the stones of the wall could speak, what a tale they would have to tell. Sky Hill was the site of a fierce battle in 1079 when the Norse king Godred Croven attacked the Manx people and defeated

CROSBY

PUBLIC TRANSPORT
Bus Douglas–Peel

SERVICES
Post Office, general store, toilets, garage

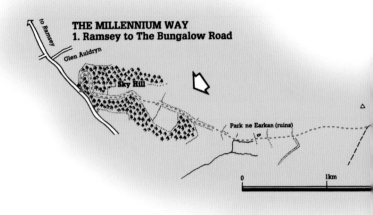

**THE MILLENNIUM WAY
1. Ramsey to The Bungalow Road**

them by clever tactics. He set an ambush then advanced with half his men. The Manx attacked from their camp on Sky Hill and drove the Norse king back to the Sulby river. As the Manx army passed the ambush they were caught between the Norsemen and the flooded river, where they surrendered. Godred spared them and took over the rule of Man, where he became a respected and much loved king.

The Way now crosses the head of Glentramman and begins to climb gently. North Barrule rises to the south-east, and in contrast to the cry of the gull the song of the skylark fills the air.

A three-way signpost clearly indicates that the Way is straight on, sharing the public footpath to the Mountain Road. From here you can just make out the cairn on the summit of North Barrule, but you can hardly miss the paraphernalia on the summit of Snaefell. Forestry work on Slieau Managh can be seen to the right and the prominent white quartzy outcrop of Creg Bedn.

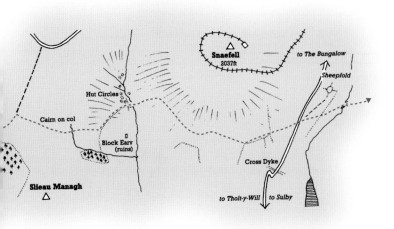

Go through the wicket gate in a stone wall, the forestry fence being on the right. The wall on the left veers off leftwards. Keep straight on to a signpost (w/m), then to a second signpost (w/m). After the second signpost the Millennium Way turns right along a less distinct track. (The path straight ahead rises steeply to join the Mountain Road.)

Sulby reservoir from the Way

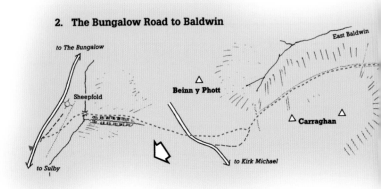

2. The Bungalow Road to Baldwin

Look ahead on the horizon where a cairn can be seen in a slight dip on the ridge. Head for it. In about 100yds a waymark appears and you are back in the old banked pathway heading for the skyline cairn.

As the cairn draws nearer and its neat shape becomes more distinct, you realise that this is no ordinary heap of stones, but a cairn of distinction. It was donated by two appreciative travellers and placed in a strategic spot as a key marker on the watershed.

Ahead now is the deep valley of Block Eary. Keep straight on down the moor. On reaching a wall turn left along it. The ruins of an old farmhouse can be seen ahead. Follow the wall as it bends (there are waymarks to guide you) to find a stile over the fence and a bridge over the stream.

This is an ideal place for a picnic directly under the summit of Snaefell (2037ft). The ancient Manx shepherds must have thought so too, for it was here that they came in summer to pasture their animals. The hummocks of earth on the left as you descended to the bridge are shielings, the remains of their summer homes. A better view of them is to be had from across the stream.

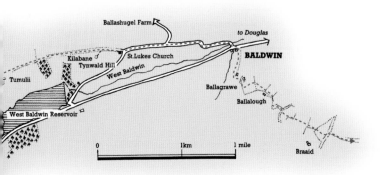

Climb steeply now across the north-west flanks of Snaefell. The path has disappeared, but the waymarks and marker poles are frequent. The path crosses a small stream and heads right (west) across a slope of rushes. (The waymark pole blends in with the background and may not be immediately apparent.) The Way is now easy to follow as it traverses Snaefell's slopes. A wall rising from the Eary valley climbs nearer then turns away. Continue to traverse as the views to the right over the forests of the Sulby valley unfold and the Sulby reservoir appears. The Way now makes for the wall, which it follows until the road is crossed and Snaefell left behind.

The road runs north-west to join the Ramsey – Kirk Michael road near Sulby village and south-east to join the Douglas–Ramsey mountain road at The Bungalow, a halt on the electric mountain railway.

You now have to lose height to cross the infant Sulby river. The path slants down leftwards by a marker pole amongst the rushes. A stile over the wire fence is the next landmark. From here spy out the route ahead, which runs up the left-hand bank of the tributary valley.

On the hillside is a circular sheepfold, best seen from the opposite fell. The four walls angled from the centre

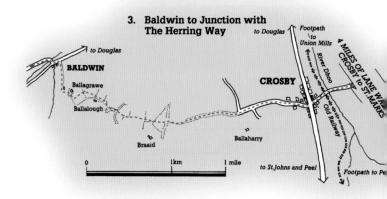

roughly correspond to the points of the compass. The workings up the valley are abandoned mines. They proved unproductive and were closed about 1867. An attractive legacy that remains is the packhorse bridge.

Cross the river by the packhorse bridge and climb steeply up the left edge of the side valley. When you need a breather turn and admire the sheepfold. I wonder how many hours of toil went into its construction? As you gain the head of the valley the old sunken track reappears. Slieau Freoghane (1601ft) and Slieau Dhoo (1417ft) stand out to the west, and Beinn-y-Phott (1791ft) to the east. An old marker stone of slate is passed on the right, and then the mountain road from Brandywell on the Douglas–Ramsey road to Kirk Michael is crossed.

The going is easy now. The track is locked between moorland embankments, and as the watershed is reached Carraghan (1640ft) rises directly in front of you.

At the next junction keep left (w/m) on the bridle track. The southern half of the island is spread out before you as the track descends through five gates to a plantation, becoming stonier as you descend.

The Millennium Way traverses farm land above Baldwin

The track (Raad Garroo – 'rough road') runs down the ridge between the West Baldwin and the East Baldwin valleys. The West Baldwin valley is lined with forest. Streams tumble noisily into the reservoir, and a quiet road creeps along the water's edge and climbs up the wooded slopes to the head of the valley.

Continue down the track, and the moment St Luke's Chapel comes into view look for an old, yet prominent stone stile on the right.

Just over the stile is Cronk Keeill Abban. The site of Tynwald 'Holden at Kil abane 1428', it is one of the three Tynwald mounds in the island. The first primitive Tynwald was described in the Sagas. The chieftain chose a mound then erected an altar to Thor. He then made a fence of tree trunks or planted trees leading to the mound. After the prayers and ceremony the chieftain would sit and listen to the woes of his subjects, pronounce his decisions and any new laws. It was here that the decision to settle quarrels by court and not by feud was initiated.

The next site of interest is St Luke's Chapel-of-Ease. The present chapel was built in 1836 on the site of the ancient Celtic church, Keeill Abban. A plaque of red sandstone is built into the gable below the bell, an ancient carved stone set in its country rock.

Beyond the chapel you join the road and bear left, walking gently downhill. Go straight on at the road junction and descend to the Baldwin valley.

Turn left over a bridge then right up a lane. The lane leads steeply up the valley side, with celandine, bluebells, primroses and the delicate yellow poppy in a springtime.

The lane bends to the left, revealing a fine view of the hills and St Luke's Chapel in its setting. At the end of the lane, go into the cottage garden to find a stile on the right leading into a field.

Look for the signpost (Millennium Way and Public Footpath) to guide you through a gate and diagonally across the field. The Way now is across the front of the farm to the right. The waymark stands in a background of trees and is not readily distinguished from this point. Pass the farm and continue along the field edge until you can go through a little green gate and stone stile by a stand of trees into a lane. Along the lane you will come to a three-way junction where you take to the fields again over a high ladder stile (w/m).

Cross two fields. The exit to the second is on the far right over a stile. The next waymark is best seen from the top of that stile, where you can plan a direct line across the field. It held a fine crop of hay when I was there. Try to maintain a single track and keep the path width to a minimum.

You are now on a lane. Turn left down the lane to join a tarmac road (w/m), which leads downhill into the Neb valley and Crosby.

Crosby to Castletown

Distance:	10½ miles
Maximum height:	473ft

Cross straight over the main road and past the park to the old railway and the river bridge.

The old railway is now a public footpath, the Heritage Way, to Peel along the pretty Neb valley, passing through St John's village and close by Tynwald Hill. It joins the Bayr ny Skeddan at Glenfaba bridge, ½

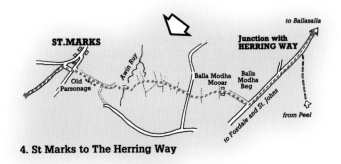

4. St Marks to The Herring Way

mile from Peel. This route is highly recommended to link the two walks into one.

The Millennium Way continues along the road for 3½ miles. At the top of the hill is Marown School, 1874, a church school of the days when children began attending at 5 years old and stayed at the same school throughout their school life.

The next site of interest is just beyond the road junction. Keep straight across, and the church on the right is St Runan's.

There has been a keeill on this site since the seventh century. Ronan or Marown was a Scottish saint, thus indicating that missionaries came to the island from Scotland.

Another ½ mile on the road will bring you to a bridle track on the right leading to St Patrick's Chair, signpost. After a few minutes' walk up the track look for a stile in the hedge on the left. St Patrick's Chair is in the centre of the field.

This is a group of standing stones, two of them carved with crosses. It is told that St Patrick preached from this spot, and that anyone who sits to rest with his back against one of the carved stones will never feel fatigued again.

The road continues to climb, passing Slieau Chiarn (636ft) on your left. As you reach the crest Castletown comes into view across the southern plain. Cross the Douglas–Foxdale road and pass by Ballacallin Mooar and Ballanicholas. You now descend to cross the Santon Burn.

Granite boulders left behind by the Ice Age glaciers were washed down by the stream and can still be seen in the river bed. Many of these boulders have been removed and incorporated into local buildings.

Cross Campbell's bridge with its interesting inscription and carry straight on at the next road junction where the Foxdale road goes off right. A mile further on is the village of St Mark's.

At a road junction turn right, then go left, cross over the road and turn right at the waymark. The lane leading past the old parsonage is lined with a variety of shrubs and is well used. It soon swings away to the right and you go straight ahead through a gate (Public Footpath sign), where it quickly deteriorates into a waterlogged and muddy track.

At the three-way signpost the Way carries straight on towards Ballamodha Road. Pause a while at the gate on the left and look ahead for two signposts on the opposite hillside to indicate your intended direction. The lane bends to a gate and stile (w/m). Cross the field and turn left along the side of the brook, which you cross by an old stone slab-bridge, and continue on the right-hand bank until you turn right over a stile (w/m). Cross diagonally left to the top corner of the field (w/m) into a green lane. The green lane is short, and the next waymark turns you right to a kissing gate in the far hedge. Go straight on across the next three fields. Cross the lane and the following field (w/ms) into an enclosed lane leading into the Ballamodha Mooar farmyard. Cross the yard into the farm lane. As you pass the next farm, Ballamodha Beg, notice the use of the granite boulders and slate in the construction of the farm buildings.

At the road turn left to meet the Bayr ny Skeddan at the Silverburn bridge.

The walk from Silverburn bridge to Castletown is described in the Bayr ny Skeddan (see page 147–9).

BAYR NY SKEDDAN:
The Herring Way
(Peel to Castletown)

Fourteen miles (approximately)

The Bayr ny Skeddan, as may be expected, begins by the harbour and kipper factory in Peel. The high chimneys carry the fumes from the diesel-burning power station which supplies electricity to the island's grid. The Way follows the River Neb upstream to Glenfaba, from where it climbs the slopes of Corrin's Hill to join the Raad ny

Fishing boats
in Peel harbour

139

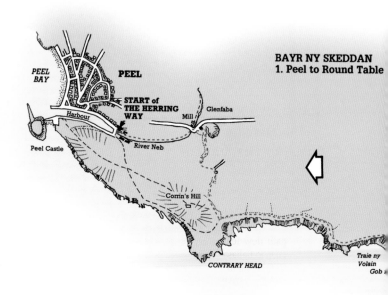

BAYR NY SKEDDAN
1. Peel to Round Table

PEEL
BAY

PEEL

PEEL

START of
THE HERRING
WAY

Glenfaba

Mill

Harbour

River Neb

Peel Castle

Corrin's Hill

CONTRARY HEAD

Traie ny
Volain
Gob

Foillan. The coastline is then followed south for 1½ miles, allowing you to enjoy the vast seascapes and admire the skill of the seabirds as they ride the updraught from the plunging cliffs. The descent into Glen Maye brings a complete contrast. The picturesque glen is followed first through a narrow verdant valley, then as it passes through forests and finally opens out onto the high moorland between Cronk ny Arrey Laa and South Barrule, and on to the watershed at The Round Table.

The Way then crosses the slopes of South Barrule high above the Cringle Reservoir. It then descends, interestingly, along old lanes and by farm paths to meet the St John's – Castletown road, the Millennium Way and the

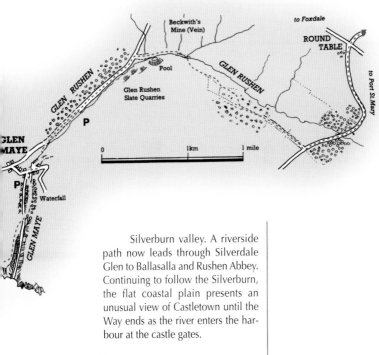

Silverburn valley. A riverside path now leads through Silverdale Glen to Ballasalla and Rushen Abbey. Continuing to follow the Silverburn, the flat coastal plain presents an unusual view of Castletown until the Way ends as the river enters the harbour at the castle gates.

Peel to Round Table

Start at the harbour bridge by a huge old anchor, attractively displayed but of unknown origin. Pass the House of Manannan, the tourist centre, which won an international award.

The fishing boats are rather strangely named. Cornishmen came to fish for herring in 1850. Their boats had a different rig to the Manx boats. Most of the Cornishmen were named Nicholas and their boats became known as 'Nickeys'. As the Manx fishermen modernised their boats in the Cornish style, they too kept the name 'Nickeys'.

The waymark is by the kipper factory fence on a signpost 'Public Footpath to Glenfaba'. Take the gruesome track between the factories, passing the power station, and put the industry of the first hundred yards of the Bayr ny Skeddan behind you.

The path takes the old railway by the River Neb.

The old mill leat is still active, bringing water to cool the power station's diesel generators. At the old disused mill across the river a small waterwheel can be seen.

The path leads under a bridge. This is Glenfaba. Just beyond the bridge is a fine pair of waterwheels, with the leat and sluices still in place. A path and steps to the right lead up onto the road bridge. Cross the river and the road, then take the lane right by the side of a cottage (w/m). The lane winds uphill leaving the Neb valley behind, and in front Corrin's Hill looks impressive. Where the lane forks keep straight uphill. The lane is now between high banks, and the nettles, flowers and trickle of water attract butterflies. As the lane bends keep left, then right, until at its end you can cross a stile on the right to the open fell on Corrin's Hill.

A panorama of mountains lies inland. To the north of St John's lie Beary Mountain (1020ft), Coldon (1599ft) and Carraghan (1640ft). In the far background is Snaefell (2036ft) framed against Sartfell (1490ft) and Slieau Freoghane (1610ft). To the south of St John's stands Slieau Whillain (1094ft) or the Witches' Hill.

Tradition tells that those suspected of witchcraft were taken to the top of the hill and placed in a barrel into which iron spikes had been driven. The barrel was then rolled down the hill. If the unfortunate victim was found to be dead at the bottom then she had received her just deserts. However, if she was still alive she was obviously a witch and was burnt at the stake.

Turn left by the wall and as the path levels out a beautiful scene appears.

The coastline hills, their foundations touched by the sea, stand looking west – Cronk ny Arrye Laa, Lhiattee ny Beinnee and Bradda Hill, with the tail of Niarbyl pointing out to sea.

At the wicket gate you join the Raad ny Foillan for a few miles. Go through the gate (w/m) and follow the coastal path south. This is a magnificent path, high above the sea. After crossing the field wall by a stile, skirting a spring and returning to the cliff top, the next headland, Gob ny Sharray, has a wide grassy crown.

Here is the place to observe the colonies of nesting herring gulls and fulmar and to encounter the stonechat. I couldn't help smiling at its call, a shrill 'peep' then 'grunt, grunt'. In spring the path is clothed with primroses and white campion. Bluebells grow, with short sturdy stems and huge flowerheads of dark purple.

Waterfall in Glen Maye

The path descends into Glen Maye. Here you part from the Raad ny Foillan and turn inland (w/m). The official route turns left up the narrow road to the Waterfall Hotel, but a better alternative is to leave the Way temporarily here to walk up the glen footpath.

Cross the road and enter the gate by the site of the Mona Erin waterwheel. A plaque on the wall tells you its history. As you progress up the glen you will appreciate that it is a place of rare beauty. Take the Waterfall Path and take your time to admire the ferns and plants in their lovely setting. A path branches left for a better view of the waterfall. Climb steeply, then cross a bridge over the stream to emerge from the gorge to meet the narrow road at the Waterfall Hotel (meals) (car park and toilets).

Cross the main road and turn right. Cross the river bridge and branch left down a small lane (waymark). Turn left again down a path at the Public Footpath sign

143

(the Postman's Path) to Glen Rushen. Keep right to gain the river bank. Cross the river and carry on upstream to join a minor road. It is now closed to traffic for a short way, with the tarmac fighting a losing battle with the grass. This leads to a parking area with picnic tables.

Across the now deepening valley, the hillside, in spring, is a carpet of bluebells. Clear streams tumble through the forest as you progress up the valley. Old slate quarry workings with their spoil heaps can be seen high on the opposite hillside.

Keep on the road, pass through the forest and fork right at the junction (w/m). An old dam on the right with a strange wire canopy is part of the Peel water supply.

Notice how the river colour changes. The River Maye ('maye' is Manx for 'yellow') has suddenly begun to live up to its name. On the hillside above was one of the principal lead mines of the island. The Foxdale vein ran for 3 miles in an east–west direction. Of the thirteen shafts sunk, Beckwith's lies just above this 'yellow outlet'.

In Glen Rushen, with the chimney of Beckwith's mine above

It was a chance discovery. A man driving his haycart noticed a mass of lead ore (galena) in the heather. The ore contained a considerable amount of silver and was worked until 1910. Beckwith's shaft reaches a depth of 1100ft, which is 500ft below sea level. The mine was closed when prices fell and the operation became uneconomic, but it is not worked out and to date licences are still held. The spoil heaps and full extent of the workings can be seen as you progress up Glen Rushen.

Cross the river by the bridge and keep to the right of the water supply catchment area. A stile and waymark direct you onto a small path running steeply up the hillside with early summer orchids on its edge. Go to the next waymark, where you can turn for a view of the mines and the slopes of South Barrule. The next stile enters the Forestry Department, Creg ny Crock. The path climbs steadily to the next waymark by an old ruined farmhouse. Turn left along the forest track. The track now crosses a few small streams as it passes through the plantation established in 1986.

The seedlings of new plantations on the island nestle in the furrows, unlike the English plantations where they are planted on the ridges. This is to protect them from the wind and to give access to any moisture available in the usually dry spring weather on the western side of the island.

A pleasant green track, with extensive views of South Barrule and Cronk ny Arrey Laa, leads to a road.

Turn left at the main road (w/m), cross over the bridge and, with South Barrule on the left and Cronk ny Arree Laa on the right, keep straight on to gain the crossroads at 'Round Table' quickly and easily.

Round Table to junction with the Millennium Way

Cross over the Port Erin – Foxdale road (w/m).

The views from here are extensive in all directions as you come over the watershed. From Glen Maye you have climbed steadily to 1000ft above sea level, and from now on it is downhill all the way.

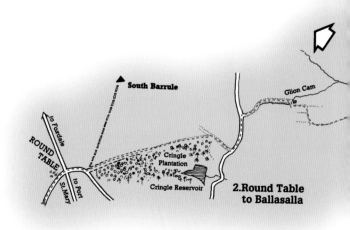

2.Round Table to Ballasalla

Turn left at the corner of the Cringle Plantation onto a stony track by the forest side. The track mounts a slight brow where a new forestry road branches right. Keep straight on. Another track joins from the right. Here you can see some quartz boulders built into the wall.

Keep straight on down the hill, with the Silverburn valley and the Cringle Reservoir on the right. At the crossroads turn left (w/m) along the road until you meet a right turn to Ballamodha Farm and Glenmoar Farm (w/m). The farm lane descends by a little stream until it flows into a busy duckpond at Old Moaney. Turn right (w/m on the barn side), then left into an enclosed lane through a gate. Keep straight on and follow the right-hand edge of the field to a stile. Public Footpath sign. Turn left along the old embanked lane and straight on through the farmyard at Moaney Mooar, where the lane becomes wider and smoother. The lane bends right then left before it joins the main road. Turn right down the hill past an old milestone to the Athol Bridge over the Silverburn.

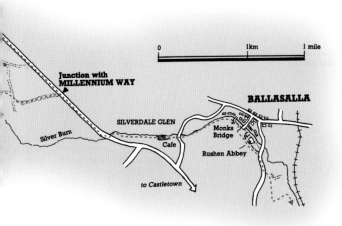

Junction with the Millennium Way

The Bayr ny Skeddan now joins the Millennium Way. What a meeting-place of travellers this must have been – a place of news and gossip as friends from the north and the west met, and a welcome rest for the pack animals while tales were told.

Cross the Athol Bridge and turn left onto the riverbank path (w/m). Cross the leat and walk between the leat and the burn through the shady woodland. Suddenly you realise that the turf is mown and the rushing leat has emptied its water into a small lake. This is Silverdale Glen. The footpath goes straight ahead past the lake.

There is a cafe in the old mill building and the waterwheel is in working order. A unique Victorian over-shot waterwheel begins to turn as water is released from the lake leat by an iron lever, which you are free to work. Its power has been harnessed to drive a carousel, which revolves at a gentle pace, its brightly painted wooden horses giving rides to the children.

147

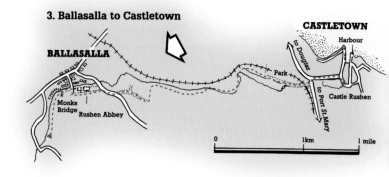

3. Ballasalla to Castletown

Exit at the glen car park by the road and regain the riverside woodland at the waymark. The footpath passes a gate at the glen entrance and you will notice from looking at the river bed that you are now in an area of limestone.

The Monks' Bridge over the Silver Burn was built by the monks of Rushen Abbey in 1350. It is a picturesque double-arched bridge paved with quartz cobbles.

Do not cross the Monks' Bridge but go straight on. At the ford the footbridge is the nearest way to the centre of Ballasalla and the shops. From the ford the footpath makes its way around the right-hand side of Rushen Abbey. ◀

The alternative option for the temporary diversion of Raad ny Fiollan joins here.

If you want to visit the ruins keep straight on.

Rushen Abbey, although small, played an important part in Manx history. In 1134 Olaf I gave permission to the Abbot of Furness Abbey to build an abbey in Ballasalla. In 1147 it came under the rule of the Cistercian Order. The monks were farmers and lived on the results of their labours. They became known as experts in land drainage, and eventually the Abbot had under his influence the best farmland, the mining and also the fishing. The

Abbot of Rushen was a baron in his own right and owned two sets of gallows where he exercised judgment over life and death. Today only a few ruins remain, although the good Norman arch of the north transept is still intact.

Beyond the Abbey cross the main road, and a short way up the hill the Bayr ny Skeddan/Millennium Way branches left. Keep straight on at the wicket gate and along the track. Turn left down a grassy path to an old ruined barn by the river (w/m). Turn right along the riverside. Just across the water is the railway, and if a train goes by you will have a grandstand view of the steaming engine. The path runs along the bank of the river until it crosses to the left bank at a bridge. Here you will have the same view of Castle Rushen as the fishermen from Peel must have looked for with anticipation. Keep straight along the path past the park. Cross the road and in a few minutes you will reach journey's end at Castletown Harbour.

The Monk's Bridge, Ballasalla

149

Castle Rushen overlooks Castletown harbour

APPENDIX 1
Glossary of Manx Words

Sc – Scandinavian origin   C – Celtic origin

Agneash (Sc)	Edge, nose
Andreas	Andrew
Ayre (Sc)	A pebbly beach
Balla (C)	Farm or homestead
Barrule (Sc)	Wardfell of ward and watch (from 'Warool')
Bradda (Sc)	Broad headland
Cass-ny-Hawin (C)	The end of the river
Cornaa (Sc)	Waterwheel
Cronk (C)	Hill
Cregneish/Creagneish (Sc)	The ness of the crows (from 'Craukness')
Dhoon (C)	Fort
Douglas (C)	The dark stream
Ellan Vannin	Isle of Man
Fleshwick (Sc)	green creek (from 'Fles-vik')
Gog (C)	Mouth
Jurby (Sc)	Invar's home (from 'Ingvar-byr')
Laxey (Sc)	Salmon river
Langness (Sc)	Long headland
Lhen (C)	A trench
Maye – Glen (C)	The yellow glen
Meayll or Mull (C)	Bare (from 'Maol')
Mooar Glen (C)	The great glen
Niarbyl (C)	The tail (from 'Yn arby')
Peel (Sc)	A fortress
Poyllvaaish (C)	Pool of death
Purt/Phurt	Harbour, port
Ramsey (Sc)	Island of garlic
Ronaldsway (C)	Ronald's boat path
Rue (C)	Red point
Santon	St Sanctain (from 'Santon')
Scarlett	Cormorants' ledge (from 'Skarfakluft')
Slieau (C)	Mountain
Soderick (Sc)	Sunny creek (from 'Sol-vik')
Sumark	Primrose
Wyllin (Glen) (C)	The mill glen

APPENDIX 2
Selected Bibliography

Airne C.W., *The Story of the Isle of Man* Vols I & 11 1964

Allan D.E., *The Flowering Plants of the Isle of Man*

Caine W. Ralph Hall, *The Isle of Man*. 1909

Corrin H.S., *The Isle of Man*. 1977

Crockett S.R., *The Raiders*. 1954

Cullen J.P. & Jennings P.P., *Birds of the Isle of Man*. 1986

Falconar A.E.I., *Celtic Tales of Myth and Fantasy*. 1984

Herbert A., *The Isle of Man*. 1909

Lockington Marshall W., *The Calf of Man*. 1978

Memoirs, *Geological Survey of Great Britain*. 1954.

Moseley, *The Geology of the Lake District*. 1978

Palmer T., *Discover the Isle of Man*. 1987

Stenning E.H., *The County Books – The Isle of Man*. 1950

Stenning E.H., *Portrait of the Isle of Man*. 1983

Reed's Nautical Almanac. 2003

APPENDIX 3
Route Summary

RAAD NY FOILLAN	Distance (miles)	Max height (ft)	Height gain (ft)
Douglas harbour to Castletown harbour Mainly clifftop footpath to Ronaldsway; road to Derby Haven and Castletown	15¼	300	750
Castletown harbour to Peel St Mary harbour Easy walking on level paths and roads, or beach	6½	sea level	negligible
Port St Mary harbour to Port Erin Road then well-trodden paths through exposed clifftop moorland	7	400	1000
Port Erin beach to Peel harbour A spectacular mountain and moorland day; some minor lane walking but mainly moorland paths	14½	1434	3018
Peel harbour to Kirk Michael Cliff path then an old railway trackbed followed by ¼ mile of beach	7½	200	200
Kirk Michael to Point of Ayre Beach and coastal heath	15	sea level	
Point of Ayre to Ramsey harbour Beach and promenade	7	sea level	
Ramsey harbour to Laxey harbour A variety of beach, road, clifftop path and glen	13	650	1524
Laxey harbour to Douglas A mixture of road, lane and track walking, clifftop fields and paths	9½	350	750
THE MILLENNIUM WAY			
Ramsey to Crosby Mountain moorland traverse on paths and bridleways	12¾	1500	2480
Crosby to Castletown Quiet lanes, farmland pastures and riverside footpaths	10½	473	600
The Heritage Way (Section from Crosby to Peel) The way follows the line of an old railway	6½		
THE HERRING WAY			
Peel harbour to Castletown Coastal paths, the ascent of river glens to a high moorland watershed and the descent of a river valley to the sea	14	900	1250

APPENDIX 4
IOM Coastal Footpath Accommodation List

This list was updated in 2007. A more comprehensive selection of B&B accommodation on the coast is available from the Tourist Office.

Douglas
B&B
A choice can be found in the Department of Tourism Holiday Guide.

Campsite
(May–Sept) Grandstand Campsite, Nobles Park Douglas IM2 4BD. Tel: 01624 842 341 (office hours) (closed during TT & Manx Grand Prix fortnight), www.douglas.org.im

Castletown
B&B
The George Hotel, The Parade, Castletown. Tel: 01624 822533
Francorchamps, Fishers Hill, Castletown. Tel: 06124 823635

Hostel and Family Rooms
King Williams College, Castletown. Send for brochure. Tel: 01624 820400, Fax: 01624 820402, Email: rooms@kwc.sch.im, website: www.kws.sch.im

Port St Mary & Peel
A choice can be found in the Department of Tourism Holiday Guide.

Surby
Mrs Fairest, Amberwell, Surby Road, Surby. Tel: 01624 834449

Dalby
B&B
Ballacallin Hotel, Dalby. Tel: 01624 842030
Mr/Mrs Cain, Cronk Moar, Dalby. Tel: 01624 842738

Peel
B&B
A choice can be found in the Dept. of Tourism Holiday Guide.

Campsite
(mid April – 30th September) Peel Camping Park, Derby Road, Peel IM5 1AG.
Tel: 01624 842341, Email: nena.faulkner@ptcorg.im

Kirk Michael
B&B
Mrs Conning, Cooil Aalin, Cannan Avenue, Kirk Michael. Tel: 01624 878156
Thie Vaynrys, 4–5 The Meadows, Kirk Michael. Tel: 01624 878682

Campsite
(April – 30th September) Glen Wyllin Campsite. Tel: 01624 878231
(Oct – Mar) Tel: 01624 878836

Jurby
B&B
Mr/Mrs Marshall, Goldies Loughan, Jurby East. Tel: 01624 897834

Ramsey
B&B
A choice can be found in the Department of Tourism Holiday Guide.

Campsite
(May–September) Crossags Campsite, Crossags Lane, Ramsey. Tel: 01624 816099

Maughold
B&B
Mrs Murray, Bwoaillee Drommey, Ballajora Hill, Maughold. Tel: 07624 812265

Hostel
Venture Centre, Lewaigue Farm, Maughold. Tel: 01624 814240

Dhoon
B&B
Ballashalogue Farm. Main Road, Glen Mona. Tel: 01624 861 750

Campsite
Dhoon Glen Campsite, Dhoon. Tel: 01624 862070

Laxey
B&B
Mrs Howarth, Narrow Gate House, Old Laxey Hill, Laxey. Tel: 01624 861966
Mrs Whelan, Marine Mount, Croit-e-Quill Road, Laxey. Tel: 01624 861714
Mrs Quirk, The Greaves, Ramsey Road, Lazey. Tel: 01624 861500

Campsite
(Easter – 30th September) Quarry Road, Laxey. Tel: 01624 862623

Onchon
B&B
A choice can be found in the Dept. of Tourism Holiday Guide.

Millennium Way
Campsite
(May–October) Glenlough Campsite, Main Road, Union Mills.
Tel: 01624 852057/822372, Email: glenloughcampsite@manx.net

LISTING OF CICERONE GUIDES

BACKPACKING AND CHALLENGE WALKING
Backpacker's Britain:
  Vol 1 – Northern England
  Vol 2 – Wales
  Vol 3 – Northern Scotland
  Vol 4 – Central & Southern
    Scottish Highlands
End to End Trail
The National Trails
The UK Trailwalker's Handbook
Three Peaks, Ten Tors

BRITISH CYCLING
Border Country Cycle Routes
Cumbria Cycle Way
Lancashire Cycle Way
Lands End to John O'Groats
Rural Rides:
  No 1 – West Surrey
  No 2 – East Surrey
South Lakeland Cycle Rides

PEAK DISTRICT AND DERBYSHIRE
High Peak Walks
Historic Walks in Derbyshire
The Star Family Walks – The Peak
  District & South Yorkshire
White Peak Walks:
  The Northern Dales
  The Southern Dales

SUMMIT COLLECTIONS
Europe's High Points
Mountains of England & Wales:
  Vol 1 – Wales
  Vol 2 – England
Ridges of England, Wales & Ireland
The Relative Hills of Britain

IRELAND
Irish Coast to Coast Walk
Irish Coastal Walks
Mountains of Ireland

THE ISLE OF MAN
Isle of Man Coastal Path
Walking on the Isle of Man

LAKE DISTRICT AND MORECAMBE BAY
Atlas of the English Lakes
Coniston Copper Mines
Cumbria Coastal Way
Cumbria Way and Allerdale Ramble
Great Mountain Days in the
  Lake District
Lake District Anglers' Guide
Lake District Winter Climbs
Lakeland Fellranger:
  The Central Fells
  The Mid-Western Fells
  The Near-Eastern Fells
  The Southern Fells
Roads and Tracks of the Lake District
Rocky Rambler's Wild Walks
Scrambles in the Lake District:
  Vol 1 – Northern Lakes
  Vol 2 – Southern Lakes

Short Walks in Lakeland:
  Book 1 – South Lakeland
  Book 2 – North Lakeland
  Book 3 – West Lakeland
Tarns of Lakeland:
  Vol 1 – West
  Vol 2 – East
Tour of the Lake District
Walks in Silverdale and Arnside

NORTHERN ENGLAND
LONG-DISTANCE TRAILS
Dales Way
Hadrian's Wall Path
Northern Coast to Coast Walk
Pennine Way
Reivers Way
Teesdale Way

NORTH-WEST ENGLAND
OUTSIDE THE LAKE DISTRICT
Family Walks in the
  Forest of Bowland
Historic Walks in Cheshire
Ribble Way
Walking in the Forest of Bowland
  and Pendle
Walking in Lancashire
Walks in Lancashire Witch Country
Walks in Ribble Country

PENNINES AND NORTH-EAST ENGLAND
Cleveland Way and Yorkshire
  Wolds Way
Historic Walks in North Yorkshire
North York Moors
The Canoeist's Guide to the
  North-East
The Spirit of Hadrian's Wall
Yorkshire Dales – North and East
Yorkshire Dales – South and West
Walking in County Durham
Walking in Northumberland
Walking in the North Pennines
Walking in the South Pennines
Walks in Dales Country
Walks in the Yorkshire Dales
Walking on the West Pennine Moors
Walks on the North York Moors:
  Books 1 and 2
Waterfall Walks – Teesdale and
  High Pennines
Yorkshire Dales Angler's Guide

SCOTLAND
Ben Nevis and Glen Coe
Border Country
Border Pubs and Inns
Central Highlands
Great Glen Way
Isle of Skye
North to the Cape
Lowther Hills
Pentland Hills
Scotland's Far North
Scotland's Far West

Scotland's Mountain Ridges
Scottish Glens:
  2 – Atholl Glens
  3 – Glens of Rannoch
  4 – Glens of Trossach
  5 – Glens of Argyll
  6 – The Great Glen
Scrambles in Lochaber
Southern Upland Way
Walking in the Cairngorms
Walking in the Hebrides
Walking in the Ochils, Campsie Fells
  and Lomond Hills
Walking Loch Lomond and the
  Trossachs
Walking on the Isle of Arran
Walking on the Orkney and Shetland
  Isles
Walking the Galloway Hills
Walking the Munros:
  Vol 1 – Southern, Central and
    Western
  Vol 2 – Northern and Cairngorms
West Highland Way
Winter Climbs – Ben Nevis and
  Glencoe
Winter Climbs in the Cairngorms

SOUTHERN ENGLAND
Channel Island Walks
Exmoor and the Quantocks
Greater Ridgeway
Lea Valley Walk
London – The Definitive Walking
  Guide
North Downs Way
South Downs Way
South West Coast Path
Thames Path
Walker's Guide to the Isle of Wight
Walking in Bedfordshire
Walking in Berkshire
Walking in Buckinghamshire
Walking in Kent
Walking in Somerset
Walking in Sussex
Walking in the Isles of Scilly
Walking in the Thames Valley
Walking on Dartmoor

WALES AND THE WELSH BORDERS
Ascent of Snowdon
Glyndwr's Way
Hillwalking in Snowdonia
Hillwalking in Wales:
  Vols 1 and 2
Lleyn Peninsula Coastal Path
Offa's Dyke Path
Pembrokeshire Coastal Path
Ridges of Snowdonia
Scrambles in Snowdonia
Shropshire Hills
Spirit Paths of Wales
Walking in Pembrokeshire
Welsh Winter Climbs

AFRICA
Climbing in the Moroccan Anti-Atlas
Kilimanjaro – A Complete Trekker's Guide
Trekking in the Atlas Mountains

THE ALPS
100 Hut Walks in the Alps
Across the Eastern Alps: The E5
Alpine Points of View
Alpine Ski Mountaineering:
    Vol 1 – Western Alps
    Vol 2 – Central & Eastern Alps
Chamonix to Zermatt
Snowshoeing: Techniques and Routes
    in the Western Alps
Tour of Mont Blanc
Tour of Monte Rosa
Tour of the Matterhorn
Walking in the Alps

EASTERN EUROPE
High Tatras
Mountains of Romania
Walking in Hungary

FRANCE, BELGIUM AND LUXEMBOURG
Cathar Way
Écrins National Park
GR5 Trail
GR20: Corsica
Mont Blanc Walks
Robert Louis Stevenson Trail
Selected Rock Climbs in Belgium and
    Luxembourg
Tour of the Oisans: The GR54
Tour of the Queyras
Tour of the Vanoise
Trekking in the Vosges and Jura
Vanoise Ski Touring
Walking in Provence
Walking in the Cathar Region
Walking in the Cevennes
Walking in the Dordogne
Walking in the Haute Savoie:
    Vol 1 – North
    Vol 2 – South
Walking in the Languedoc
Walking in the Tarentaise and
    Beaufortain Alps
Walking the French Gorges
Walking on Corsica
Walks in Volcano Country

FRANCE AND SPAIN
Canyoning in Southern Europe
Way of St James – France
Way of St James – Spain

GERMANY AND AUSTRIA
Germany's Romantic Road
King Ludwig Way
Klettersteig – Scrambles in
    Northern Limestone Alps
Trekking in the Stubai Alps
Trekking in the Zillertal Alps
Walking in Austria
Walking in the Bavarian Alps
Walking in the Harz Mountains
Walking in the Salzkammergut
Walking the River Rhine Trail

HIMALAYA
Annapurna: A Trekker's Guide
Bhutan
Everest: A Trekker's Guide
Garhwal & Kumaon: A Trekker's and
    Visitor's Guide
Kangchenjunga: A Trekker's Guide
Langtang with Gosainkund and
    Helambu: A Trekker's Guide
Manaslu: A Trekker's Guide
Mount Kailash Trek

ITALY
Central Apennines of Italy
Gran Paradiso
Italian Rock
Shorter Walks in the Dolomites
Through the Italian Alps: The GTA
Trekking in the Apennines
Treks in the Dolomites
Via Ferratas of the Italian
    Dolomites:
    Vols 1 and 2
Walking in Sicily
Walking in the Central Italian Alps
Walking in the Dolomites
Walking in Tuscany

MEDITERRANEAN
High Mountains of Crete
Jordan – Walks, Treks, Caves, Climbs
    and Canyons
Mountains of Greece
The Ala Dag (Turkey)
Treks and Climbs Wadi Rum, Jordan
Walking in Malta
Western Crete

NORTH AMERICA
Grand Canyon with Bryce and Zion
    Canyons
John Muir Trail
Walking in British Columbia

THE PYRENEES
GR10 Trail: Through the
    French Pyrenees
Mountains of Andorra
Rock Climbs in the Pyrenees
Pyrenees – World's Mountain Range
    Guide
The Pyrenean Haute Route
Through the Spanish Pyrenees: GR11
Walks and Climbs in the Pyrenees

SCANDINAVIA
Pilgrim Road to Nidaros
    (St Olav's Way)
Walking in Norway

SLOVENIA, CROATIA AND MONTENEGRO
Julian Alps of Slovenia
Mountains of Montenegro
Trekking in Slovenia
Walking in Croatia

SOUTH AMERICA
Aconcagua

SPAIN AND PORTUGAL
Costa Blanca Walks:
    Vol 1 – West
    Vol 2 – East

Mountains of Central Spain
Picos de Europa
Via de la Plata (Seville to Santiago)
Walking in Madeira
Walking in Mallorca
Walking in the Algarve
Walking in the Canary Islands:
    Vol 1 – West
    Vol 2 – East
Walking in the Cordillera Cantabrica
Walking in the Sierra Nevada
Walking the GR7 in Andalucia

SWITZERLAND
Alpine Pass Route
Bernese Alps
Central Switzerland
Tour of the Jungfrau Region
Walking in the Valais
Walking in Ticino
Walks in the Engadine

INTERNATIONAL CYCLING
Cycle Touring in France
Cycle Touring in Spain
Cycle Touring in Switzerland
Cycling in the French Alps
Cycling the Canal du Midi
Cycling the River Loire – The Way
    of St Martin
Danube Cycle Way
Way of St James – Le Puy to Santiago

MINI GUIDES
Avalanche!
First Aid and Wilderness Medicine
Navigating with GPS
Navigation
Snow

TECHNIQUES AND EDUCATION
Beyond Adventure
Book of the Bivvy
Map and Compass
Mountain Weather
Moveable Feasts
Outdoor Photography
Rock Climbing
Snow and Ice
Sport Climbing
The Adventure Alternative
The Hillwalker's Guide to
    Mountaineering
The Hillwalker's Manual

For full and up-to-date information
on our ever-expanding list of guides,
please visit our website:
www.cicerone.co.uk.

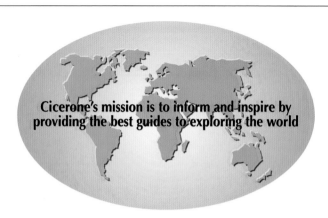

Cicerone's mission is to inform and inspire by providing the best guides to exploring the world

Since its foundation 40 years ago, Cicerone has specialised in publishing guidebooks and has built a reputation for quality and reliability. It now publishes nearly 300 guides to the major destinations for outdoor enthusiasts, including Europe, UK and the rest of the world.

Written by leading and committed specialists, Cicerone guides are recognised as the most authoritative. They are full of information, maps and illustrations so that the user can plan and complete a successful and safe trip or expedition – be it a long face climb, a walk over Lakeland fells, an alpine cycling tour, a Himalayan trek or a ramble in the countryside.

With a thorough introduction to assist planning, clear diagrams, maps and colour photographs to illustrate the terrain and route, and accurate and detailed text, Cicerone guides are designed for ease of use and access to the information.

If the facts on the ground change, or there is any aspect of a guide that you think we can improve, we are always delighted to hear from you.

Cicerone Press
2 Police Square Milnthorpe Cumbria LA7 7PY
Tel: 015395 62069 Fax: 015395 63417
info@cicerone.co.uk www.cicerone.co.uk

CICERONE